The Divine Child

The Divine Child

Your Soul's Inner Voice

By Dr. Emma Farr Rawlings

Waterside Press

Waterside Press
Cardiff by the Sea, CA, USA
ISBN: 978-1-939116-72-7
Published 2018

DISCLAIMER

Cover Design: KLD Design
Editing: Cynthia Kane, Jennifer McKinley, Sheri Hanlon
Author's photo: Smeeta Mahanti

Advance Praise

The Divine Child is awe-inspiring! Finally, out of the mouths of *The Divine Child* comes the Voice of our Soul, opening us again to the love, wisdom, and wonderment of childhood. Dr. Emma Farr Rawlings gives us a magical yet real glimpse into her life and that of children from around the world, to help us all become better humans able to help the children in our lives, which in turn helps Mother Earth. It is a timely gift from heaven to a confused and perplexed humanity. It opens doors never before opened. Scientists and laymen alike will find new ways to tap into the secrets of the universe. Many readers may rediscover a paradise lost, the age of peace and harmony when humanity had respect and love for one another – and for our one-of-a-kind, life-supporting Earth.

With an elegant combination of humor, love, and professional skill, the author interviews children of ages four to twelve. Hidden in the depths of their young hearts she finds, and taps into, the wisdom of their souls. A must read!

– Claes Nobel, The New Nobel Legacy: Earth Ethics Prize, United Earth.

This book is a treasured gift retracing our deepest remembrance of who we are, and the forever magical children around us and inside of us.

How timely to read these stories that Dr. Farr Rawlings has presented, when humanity needs to reconnect inwardly and with the magnificent, but gravely endangered, planet. The youth are our future and provide clear wisdom, love and imagination to help guide us forward at this critical time.

    – Osprey Orielle Lake, Founder and Executive Director of the Women's Earth and Climate Action Network, and author of the award-winning book, *Uprisings for the Earth: Reconnecting Culture with Nature.*

This book brings to life ancient wisdom and strength from the mouths of babes. Through her own childhood experiences and interviews with children around the world, Emma Farr Rawlings provides a glimpse into the special relationship that children have with Spirit. We are reminded that we are all a spark of the divine – we exist before physical birth and after death. The wisdom, imagination and basic goodness that flows through the children in *The Divine Child* is much needed medicine for the world on how to be with one another and nature.

    – Philip M. Hellmich, Director of Peace, The Shift Network, Author of *God and Conflict: A Search for Peace in a Time of Crisis.*

Dr. Farr Rawlings has written a timely and most needed book to inspire us to rediscover the magic of the child within all of us. It's clearly written, blending wisdom, humor and creativity drawn from her own childhood experience as well as the interviews of children from all across the globe. This book will delight you and stimulate your desire to reconnect to the wisdom, humor and joy of your own inner child. It captures one's imagination to reflect and review one's own childhood touching on the surprises and delights of one's inner divinity and love. A lovely, sweet and enticing read; a gift for us all.

– Ronald A. Alexander Ph.D., Author of *Wise Mind Open Mind* and Executive Director of the Open Mind Training Institute, Santa Monica, CA.

The Divine Child is an inspired book that only Dr. Emma Farr Rawlings could have written. She brings intelligence and gentle humor to her own stories and to her interviews with children about life's biggest mysteries. Her distinct gift for listening to and seeing others gives us a powerful book about intuition, magic and the profound wisdom of the next generation. She shows that we're in good hands!

– Wynn Burkett, Author of *Life After Baby*, Founder, The Golden Gate Mother's Group.

Dr. Emma Farr Rawlings shares a lifetime of knowing, seeing, feeling and exploring how to engage the world in new ways. Through her stories and experiences in understanding the wisdom of children, we can better comprehend how to reawaken the quieted voice inside us that once knew that the world holds magic, love and endless possibilities. It's a workbook for the soul.

– Patti Clauson, Mother, Artist, Activist.

Everywhere we look, we see the need for divine parents to produce divine children. In general, divine behavior requires only love – the desire to do good to others. If you have a desire to do good and never to do harm to yourself and to others, you are an example of divinity. In this delightful book *The Divine Child*, Emma Farr Rawlings provides a breadth of stories that exemplify the divine life. It is indeed a heart-warming experience which will encourage everyone to continue the divine experience of a happy, healthy human life.

– C. Norman Shealy, M.D., Ph.D., Author of *Conversations with G: A Physician's Encounter with Heaven*, President of International Institute of Holistic Medicine.

Dr. Emma Farr Rawlings, makes her deep grasp of childhood, and the child within, accessible at this precise moment we need to stop and listen to children everywhere, across the globe. What a gift it is to have this book appear when it is painfully clear that so many institutions tasked with teaching and protecting children are, in fact, failing them instead. These stories of young people and their wise knowing is the very antidote we need now. Listen to the children and most importantly, believe them! What if we believed what children tell us about their lives? What if we treated them with the respect we want ourselves? What if we believed the voice of the child within ourselves? The world would indeed be transformed. It's the children who are leading the way – on gun control, on voting rights, on non-violence, on racial justice, and on climate change.

– China Galland, Author of: *Love Cemetery;* and *Longing for Darkness: Tara and the Black Madonna.* Visionary and Producer, *Resurrecting Love.* Associate of the Society of the Sacred Heart, RSCJ.

As children of the Earth, we are equal stewards of our planet, including all living beings upon it. Each one of us has the opportunity to care for many children – our inner child, the child-like innocence of Nature, and the people with whom we share this magnificent home. Let us humbly remember this and simply love. Through its immense heart and deep insight into the wisdom inherent in children, Dr. Emma Farr Rawlings's book inspires wonderment and possibility for a better world.

– Parvati, Award-winning Musician, Yogini, Author and Founder of Parvati.org; dedicated to a healthy world.

Knowing Emma for many, many years it is unquestionable that she put her heart and her soul into this book and those reading it will feel an awakening of their own. The Divine Homesickness so prevalent in us in the Western world today will have a moment of redemption and a feeling of belonging once again; our existential lack of meaning will be replaced by a sense of remembering; our experience of potential and limitless possibility will be renewed. And we will welcome these, as one welcomes the morning sunrise, the birth of a child, the emergence of a new idea, and the moment we know that we are loved and whole.

– Lady Diana Whitmore, Author, Social Activist, Founder of charities aiming to put the soul back into both psychology and into the everyday life of those who suffer.

This book has a profound universal resonance. It speaks to the soul's original knowledge, still held accessible when we are young children. If we embraced and nurtured this awareness from the very beginning of life, what kind of a future world would be inherited? We must never turn our backs on our true nature. Bravo!

– Sally A Ranney, Environmental Strategist and Visionary.

Emma Farr Rawlings has interviewed young children about their unfathomable origin (ours too): where were they before they were born? Where does everything come from? In this book she has published their answers, together with a few memories from her own childhood. Her world, like the one of the children she interviews, is full of surprises and mysteries. If you read this book, be ready to abandon the reassuring support of logic and common sense, and to navigate in a world full of wonders. Also, the children's lively answers may very well put you back in touch with the eternal child in yourself.

One thing is for sure, the author gives an ear to the voices we most need to hear: the voices of children.

– Piero Ferrucci, Author of *What Our Children Teach Us.*

Dr. Farr Rawlings has eloquently reminded global citizens to return to their 'roots' of *The Divine Child* within. Her timely words nurture our universal soul, and remind us of the seeds we have in common rather than those which separate us. This book is a gift, and transcends borders with the power of love and abundant possibilities. As a Mother and Grandmother, this book is a treasure for future generations.

– Heidi Kuhn, Founder and CEO, Roots of Peace.

Inspirational friend and wise colleague, Emma has been interviewing children almost her entire life, and digs deep into the original godness and innate intelligence within each and all of their hearts and souls, and ours – unveiling endangered natural resources – including innocence and acceptance, resilience, forgiveness, creativity, gentleness – and the inexhaustible playfulness of loving grounded in our own incorruptible, innate divine nature. We are all like Buddhas by nature, young and old, sleeping buddhas and awakened ones: what we 'be' prior to and upstream from the flow of what we do, fabricate, achieve and become. Viewed through the lens of her personal story, research, interviews, and experience, here we find windows to the soul, portals to seeing the light in each and all of us. Making the future brighter and this entire interdependent natural world a much better place for generations to come.

– Lama Surya Das, Author of bestselling book, *Awakening the Buddha Within*, and founder of the Dzogchen Meditation Center for Buddhism in the West.

With *The Divine Child*, Dr. Rawlings has given us all a priceless gift: a book that sweeps us away to a realm where everything is possible and nothing is out of reach. Every page is filled with the wisdom of innocence. It is a world that is fresh and guileless, unfiltered and free. If you let it, this book will take you and your inner child on an enchanted journey neither one of you will ever forget.

The Divine Child proves what futurist Buckminster Fuller so wisely pointed out: because our children were born into a more evolved reality, they are our elders, in Universe time.

– Neal Rogin, Author, *The Delightment*, multi award winning writer and filmmaker.

*"We must rekindle our knowing of a personal
power that can flow with the power of all things
and never be exhausted."*

– Joseph Chilton Pearce

For my son Patrick, thank you for choosing me as your mom, and

for your encouragement,

music, laughter, and wisdom.

I love you so.

For my husband Sir Jimmy, I am so glad we met.

For my mom Hope, thank you for letting me BE.

For my dad Wayne, thank you for saying goodbye in my dream.

For my stepdad Jim, your sense of fun, giving me even more hope.

For my brother Geoff, your poems and love.

For my brother Jim, your constant search for the truth.

For my brother Jeff, Batman Forever.

For my sister, my best friend, my Jan.

For dear Georgia, your huge beautiful heart.

For my godchildren Dustin, Maxine, Amber, Paris, Yolanda,

Olive, and Kristy.

For Brett, Timmy, Lam, Jake, Ron, Mathieu, Neal, Philip, Claes,

Winkie, Al, Surya, Piero, Quoc, Marcus, Eric, Mac, Aron,

Chip,

Phoenix, Howard, Norm, Ayo, Steven, Harry, Andy, Daniel,

Gerald, Jon, Joe, Larry, Henk, Paul, John, Ben, Rishi, Dave, Mike,

Sunny,

Pam, Diana, Betsy, Dory, Patti, Sally, Sue, Leo, Carol,

Hiu, Lydia, Muriel, Lila, Lori, Wynn, Erin, Gail, Ro, Audrey,

Becky, Eve, Shelly, Hanieh, Susan, Diane, Kyleigh, Lisa,

Robin,

Osprey, Gorica, Gunda, Heidi, Lee, Marjorie, Kira, Parvati,
Ayrin, Patsy, Jennifer, Mihaela, Marsha, Chrissie, Bobbi, Doris,
Consuelo, Margaretha, Jayni, Stina, Sylvy, Jana, Mariam, Nancy,
Graciela, Jean, China, Barbara, Julie, and
Mary.
For all the children of war, refugee camps, violence, holocaust
survivors, natural disasters, those suffering at any border,
Mother Earth,
Endless Love.

"The unknown energy that can help humanity is that which lies hidden in the child."

– Maria Montessori

Table of Contents

"When a human is born, they're already filled with an intuitive knowledge of centuries and centuries of people beforehand. A child has wisdom. Their cells have wisdom."

– Bruce Lipton

Author's Note

The book you are about to read is a collection of some of my childhood experiences, some traumatic and some magical, along with interviews to show the innate wisdom children possess. It is my hope that as you read this book, you might begin to see the divine wisdom inside yourself and find solutions and guidance by reconnecting with your soul's inner voice – the child within.

I interviewed my first child when I was twelve. The child, Brett, was my neighbor and he was four years old. He was the brother of one of my best girlfriends growing up who lived across the street. My girlfriend was staying with us the day Brett was born. I recall my mom taking us to see Brett in the hospital just hours later. We were looking in through the glass at little babies and suddenly a nurse brought this adorable, red, mushed-up face with mounds of wet, black hair up close to the window. I felt such love for this little creature that had just arrived on earth. I was kind of a little jealous he was not my baby brother, but I was happy for my girlfriend.

My mom and I both recall to this day that Brett would cry a great deal but when I was with him, he calmed down. It became noted that Brett and I had a unique relationship and indeed we did. Even his mom would come when nothing would calm him down and put him in my lap and suddenly he was relaxed. Also, when playing over at my girlfriend's house, Brett would seek me out to be with me.

One day when Brett was old enough to really talk, he told me that he recalled me from the spirit house in the sky. I have always believed that children have innate wisdom. And I believe it's because of this knowing and the respect I have for them that when meeting and interviewing children, they open up and truly show how creative, intelligent, magical, and wise they are.

I have included Brett's interview with other interviews from children around the world in the last part of the book to really show how in sync we all were at that age to our inner voice, to our inner knowing. I also include several texts I received from Brett over 50 years later, as I needed to contact him regarding using his name in this book. I asked him a few questions as I was curious if anything from the interview still rang true to him, or even if he recalled me and maybe remembered us talking. Brett's interview at age four and his replies to my questions via text are a clear demonstration that children know and have wisdom deep within their souls at a very young age, and often retain this knowing into adulthood.

It is my hope that you will learn from my personal experience and from reading the children's interviews from around the world that children are bright, creative, spiritual beings from birth, and have a knowing about the world. They are open spiritually and carry the magic of wonder from a very young age. What I find particularly fascinating is the consistency in the children's answers from interviews conducted over five decades ago to interviews conducted in the present day. I hope that this book will raise awareness about the innate knowing that children possess so that we as a civilization might begin to care, honor and cherish our dear children on this Earth in ways that they deserve. I know if we give children love and let them know we respect their true nature, they will grow up respecting themselves, and thus will be better stewards of Earth as the Divine Child knows we are one with nature.

Dr. Emma Farr Rawlings
Northern California

"Children understand very well that in each woman, in each man, in each child, there is capacity of waking up, of understanding and of loving."

– Thich Nhat Hanh

The Big What Ifs

WHAT IF we can actually help and hear our children and their voices on any subject of their concern.

WHAT IF we can heal or comfort our own inner child's wounds so that we are healthier adults more able to serve this planet more fully?

I know from personal and professional experience we can do all of the above if we commit to doing so.

If we can pause, really listen, and help children express their true voice and experience, then we are helping the planet evolve into a healthier planet that creates a next generation that desires to do good and works toward betterment for all.

The references provided here will help give voice to all children's needs, including your own inner child. The quotes included may appear random or to be floating but they aren't. What they're doing is working toward reawakening your Divine Child.

By raising the quality of caring and consciousness of children and your own inner child, you raise the consciousness of humanity, which betters this amazing planet, Earth.

"Stop acting so small. You are the universe in ecstatic motion."

– Rumi

Part One: My Experience

"I think people should wonder about the nature of heaven and the mystical realm. But more than wonder about it, I believe that human beings are born with an innate desire – if not craving – to experience genuine sacred awe in our lives. We do not want to believe that life is random and that we evaporate at the end and that none of our choices really matter. The angelic realm is an expression of the truth that we reside in a universe that is essentially holy and sacred. We reside in the physical world for a very brief amount of time but we dwell in the spiritual world eternally."

– Caroline Myss

Little Girl in Nature

Little Girl in Magic

I can recall loving nature; the smells, colors, the light from a very young age.

I think my first memory is between about eight months and one year old. My mom would put me out on the lawn to rest or sleep on a blanket. Sometimes I was in a playpen. I might have been younger. I am not sure. I can recall my terry cloth, baby-soft clothes and my mom placing me down on the earth. I walked at nine months, so maybe I was younger, as I remember crawling on the grass and breathing in its sweet smell of soil. I was intoxicated with that smell. I was looking at birds, ladybugs and watching butterflies. I felt no separation between the earth and me. I felt as if I was part of the earth, part of the sky and clouds.

My mom says that at age two I would often drag a chair from our dining room table to the front door, climb up and unlatch the lock. I would put the chair aside and go out the front door, often into the front or back garden. I knew I wanted outside.

I felt at peace and deeply calm there.

I saw lights and colors more when I was outside. My body often felt as if I had no body, as if I was the grass, the soil, the sky. It is here I felt most at home.

I simply wanted to breathe, to smell and feel close to God.

It is here in nature where I began to have conversations directly with God other than in my nightly prayers.

It is here that I believed and knew anything was possible.

If the grass and clouds were part of me, like my arms and feet, then I could ask them to move just like asking my feet to move when I wanted to run. Out in nature, there was no time. I found my time in our garden magical.

I was one with nature and felt as if I was loved and in love all at the same time.

Nature was by far my favorite place to be.

Reader:

- Can you recall a time in your childhood when you were in nature and felt at one with your surroundings, whether that be your garden, the beach, mountains…?

- Or, if you were in the city with not much nature nearby, do you remember playing on a playground and feeling the wind or sun on your face?

- How can you now let yourself experience more time in nature, regardless of where you are, even in a city? Especially now with so much technology our human need for nature and the outdoors is even more urgent to create a balance within our lives and whole beings.

- How can you help your children and students experience more nature and learn from the earth?

- Even now with more technology being created and apps to help children learn about nature we must also breathe fresh air and help children play in the sunshine along with technology.

- What can you do today to help kids get into nature, to feel and breathe it into their lungs?

- What can you do for yourself today? Committing to more hikes, walks or simply sitting or working in your garden?

- What did your local indigenous elders know about nature that kept harmony and balance on the earth and in their souls?

"The great heroes and heroines of our society are of course the teachers, and in particular the teachers of kids in their first years. Once a child has been shown what the natural world is, it will live with them forever."

– David Attenborough

Little Girl

Big PTSD

When I was three years old looking out my bedroom window to the house next door, I witnessed my babysitter, who lived next door, tragically being stabbed to death. This traumatic event froze a part of me. It would unknowingly plague me on and off throughout my life. Only now after all these years can I see the full impact of this event. Because I was afraid of having the murderer find and kill me, I found ways to live a life flying under the radar. Of course, not all of my life choices came from this fear, but this fear played a role in my not choosing to publish this book 40 years ago, and in making some career choices. It's important to Feel and Remember a traumatic event and then *let it go*! We have traumatic events that happen throughout our life ... *all of us* ... some may seem like more or less, but we all have them.

We must help ourselves and our children know we are more than these events and feelings.

But first, we must:

Accept feelings around the traumatic event.

Feel feelings; observe memories.

Breathe five times and repeat to ourselves:

"I have feelings and memories and I am not my feelings and memories."

Breathe.

"I am I."

Breathe.

Repeat…

*Breathing and Stress Reduction Exercise created by Roberto Assagioli.

Reader:

- If memories or flashbacks continue, seek help from an experienced PTSD therapist (EFT).*

- Mindfulness training for children and meditation will help reduce stress and anxiety. See referral.*

- The Hawn Foundation by Goldie Hawn, Mind Up, a product of the Hawn Foundation, gives children skills, tools, and practices that help them navigate and thrive in today's world.

- The David Lynch Foundation by David Lynch, brings meditation to children at risk and in trauma all around the world. "I started Transcendental Meditation in 1973 and have not missed a single meditation since. Twice a day, every day. It has given me effortless access to unlimited reserves of energy, creativity, and happiness deep within. This level of life is sometimes called a 'pure consciousness'. It is a treasury. And this level of life is deep within us all. But I had no idea how powerful and profound this technique could be until I saw first-hand how it was being practiced by young children in inner city schools, veterans who suffer the living hell of post-traumatic stress disorder and women and girls who are victims of terrible violence."

- Dr. Quoc Vo D.O., How To Handle Your Feelings. Your Gut Feeling:
  http://www.youtube.com/watch?v=xJgBpFsLlG8

- Patrick Rawlings, Stress Reduction Music:
  www.earthsoundmedia.com

- Call emergency services too, if needed. There are many resources and excellent referrals.

- Have hope; know there is a light at the end of the tunnel.

- Know that PTSD can be very tricky as our whole being wants us to forget completely what happened, and we do forget until a memory or flashback happens ... but then sometimes we forget the flashbacks.

- Also, the experience of fear can be addictive. Watch out for this one. Breathe and refocus.

- Keep moving forward and have compassion for yourself as you move away from fear.

  *List of referrals in the back of the book for both children and adults.

"The wound is the place where the Light enters you."

– Rumi

Little Voice

Big Policeman

I just learned about this next piece this past week from my mom. Thank God she is still alive at age 92 and can tell me this.

I was asking her about what she remembered about me after the murder I witnessed. She said, "You were frustrated."

Wow, for all of my hypnosis and healing work about this event, I never knew I was frustrated. I do have a memory of an intense dislike for the policeman that came to our home after the murder. I have a recollection of being focused on his being so tall, wearing these huge black boots, and he had a very red face. I remember feeling a bit mad with him about something, but figured it was my displaced anger toward the man that had just murdered my babysitter. My mom said when the policeman asked if we had seen anything next door, or heard anything, I tried to tell the policeman what I had heard and seen. I was surprised by this as I thought that I was not yet talking. My mom said I was an early talker. She said several times I tried to say what I had heard and seen. I wept in relief to hear this. I had always seen myself standing up on a chair looking into my neighbor's window and then feeling that I froze in complete fear when I saw my babysitter being stabbed to death. I

12

do recall that my breathing stopped. I do not recall screaming for help, which my mom says I did. I guess this is why my mom called the police. My mom said she too tried to get the police to listen to me, but he dismissed me for being a young child.

The boy-man who stabbed my babysitter came to our front door the next day and peered into our front window. I recall running to get my mom. She called the police. The same policeman came. He said there was no way that the murderer would have come back. I do remember this. I recall the policeman said to stay in and keep the door locked just in case.

I know we did not keep our door locked for long and we were living a never-to-be-normal life from that day onward. Only looking back can I see this. At the time, I did not say to myself I had to hide this event from my life. It simply disappeared.

Then one day while playing at my girlfriend's house down the block in her bedroom we heard a noise, looked up and, at the window, was the boy-man that killed my babysitter. We ran to get her mom. The police came. This time it was a different policeman. He looked around her backyard and then said everything was okay. He gave me the impression that he thought maybe we were inventing what we had seen because I lived next door to the murder. I knew what I had seen was real or at least he was real to me. Honestly, looking back, maybe he was a flashback of the boy-man coming back to our home the day after the murder. I do not know. I do know I still have flashbacks of a boy-man looking in my front door window of wherever I am staying. It's almost so familiar to me now that I do not even recognize it as happening except I do, then I breathe and go about my day.

Reader:

- It's important to note that even with the trauma I experienced, I was able to stay with my knowing and ask for help. Please listen to kids when they speak up. This could be the trauma of being teased at school or another event but listen and take their words to heart and help them. If this brings up any memories from your past as an adult, please seek help and see the referral list attached.

- "If every eight year old in the world is taught meditation, we will eliminate violence from the world within one generation." – Dalai Lama

"You must be the change you wish to see in the world."

– Mahatma Gandhi

Three Little Dreams

Three Big Miracles

Once upon a time before age five, I think about four years old, I was still sucking my thumb and my thumb had a wart on it. My parents tried everything to get the wart off: topical medicine, a shot into the wart, covering it for days ... but nothing would make it go away. It was bleeding and troublesome; otherwise I think my parents would not have cared. One night it dawned on me that I had not asked God to remove my wart. So that night, I asked God in my bedtime prayers to please remove my wart. That night I dreamt that there was a big sky with big white fluffy clouds and lots of light coming from behind the clouds. Suddenly, and with ease, God's arm came out of the clouds and his hand held my hand with the wart on my thumb. In the morning, I woke with excitement and knew the wart was gone. And it was.

Once upon a time, it was the night before kindergarten and I had not learned to tie my shoes. I really wanted to tie my shoelaces and had tried with no luck. In my prayers, I asked God to help me please tie my shoelaces. That night I had the same dream with the sky and clouds and God's hand reaching down and guiding my hands with my shoelaces several times ... showing me how to make a bow. I woke with excitement and ran to my shoes and put them on and tied my shoelaces, and then that morning went happily to kindergarten.

Once upon a time, a new friend moved in across the street. I was about eight years old. The new girl would put on her skates and glide down the street back and forth. I just watched as I did not know how to skate. That night I asked God in my prayers to please help me skate. The same hands came down from the sky but this time he lifted me out of bed and put me right into a pair of skates on the sidewalk in front of my house. God's hands held my body and just pushed me along the sidewalk until I felt confident and reached out with my foot and began skating. Then God let me go and I skated alone with such happiness! The next morning before school, I put on my skates and skated out on the sidewalk. I did not think about it. I just knew how to skate and did. That afternoon, I told the new girl across the street that I could skate, and so we skated together and became best friends. Eventually our parents wed, and we became sisters too.

Reader:

- Can you help yourself and the children in your life learn to access infinity and beyond by joining the right and left brain with hands together in meditation and prayer?

- Are you open to miracles?

"Back of every creation, supporting it like an arch, is faith. Enthusiasm is nothing; it comes and goes. But if one believes, then miracles occur."

– Henry Miller

Dancing Angels

It was Christmas Eve. I was about four years old.

My dad and I were standing at the back of the church watching the Christmas Eve play.

I heard music and saw angels flying out of each stained-glass window, coming together in the center over our heads. I was looking for the wires to see how they were held up from the ceiling.

I could not see wires but could see the blue light and design of the angels' wings, so vibrant and golden bright blue. Their hair was bright golden like the sunshine.

I asked my dad to lift me higher, so I could see them dancing. He did.

I knew I wanted to be an angel in the play next year.

The next day at church service, I went looking in the closets of the church to find the angel costume. I could not find the costumes. I went to the coffee social where my mom was standing talking to her friends and tugged at her dress asking her where the angel costumes were.

She told me to ask her friend. I did. The friend laughed and thought I was being cute as she said there were no angels in the play last night. My heart sank; I felt sad but knew I had seen angels.

Another time I was sitting at this meditation mountain overlook. It was at a family camp we attended every year. A white glowing angel appeared and simply hovered in between the trees for about one hour. I felt great peace and love in my heart.

I was in meditation and lying down on my back. Suddenly many angels appeared. I watched them, and they were very similar to the ones that danced from the church windows. I was older – in my mid-teens. The detail of their wings was like that of butterflies, so intricate. The light was so soft and bright. The angels were so beautiful I really did not want to leave them, but I eventually decided to move from my meditation.

Reader:

- Have you seen or heard angels?

- How can we be more open and know they are here to help us?

- Have you had experiences with children where they have told you what they see or hear and maybe you did not believe them?

- Can you be open to really listening to children about their experiences, even if the experience is different from yours?

- Can you be respectful of children's ability to experience angels or otherworldly things?

"There is room in the human heart for all the divinities."

– Isabel Allende

Big Dream

Little Girl

Age Seven

I am sitting on some stone or marble steps outside the Light Temple. The air is warm, the sky blue. Everyone is dressed in biblical clothes. It looks like the pictures I see in the Bible. Almost like a Bible Disneyland. Everyone is dressed in robes and sandals. I feel the warm sun on my body. I am watching a marketplace with food and flowers.

As I am looking at the marketplace, I see my dad dressed in robes, walking with someone that looks like Jesus and another man. My dad is in the middle as they walk through the street in my direction. My dad smiles and calls out to me and I run to greet him just like he is walking in the door coming home from work. I run into his arms, he hugs me and whispers in my ear "Just remember everything is okay and is going to be okay." We hug, and he throws me on his shoulders, so I can see more as we walk. The colors in the marketplace are so vibrant. We walk toward the temple steps and my dad lifts me off his shoulders, we hug, and he sets me back down on the Light Temple's steps. We hug goodbye and he walks back away from me with the men.

Just as he is walking away, someone is trying to wake me from my dream.

I am so peaceful that I do not want to leave my dream. Someone keeps shaking my body until I wake. As I open my eyes, I see that it's my aunty, and she whispers into my ear that my dad has gone to Heaven. I think to myself, "Well I know that I just saw my dad and everything is going to be okay."

I carried this dream and my sad, weeping heart with me into my dad's funeral and still to this day I carry his whisper in my ear into all of my life's challenges. It has allowed me to stay positive and keep perspective in very hard times. There is always a soft, clear light of love in the darkest hours.

I ask myself, "Was this my father coming to say goodbye in the only way he could since he was in a hospital, miles away? Was this the strong bond of love between father and daughter, that quantum physics explains and supports? Was this my intuition or was I picking up that my father was passing? Was it all of these things?"

Reader:

- Are children more open to a psychic awareness? If so, how can we ensure that this gift in children is protected and nurtured? Encouraged even?

- For ourselves, as adults, how can we be more open at any age? How can we carry our "childlike" intuition and wisdom into our adult selves?

- Have you ever had a similar dream or experience? If so, when? As a child?

- What if we all knew in our core that everything was going to be okay? What if we made choices from trust and not from fear?

"Faith is taking the first step even when you don't see the whole staircase."

– Martin Luther King, Jr.

Little Psychic

Big Research

My mother tells me about me calling her into my room to look at the fish swimming under my bed. I do not have a memory of them under my bed, but I do remember many brightly colored fish swimming in the air above my bed at night and during the day. I always saw auras and thought everyone saw auras and that it wasn't unusual, until one day at the dinner table where everyone was gathered, my mom spoke about an article she read in the newspaper about a new camera that took photos of auras at UCLA. She said they were doing research there and she was so interested in the article. I recall saying it was not such a big deal as I saw colors around people's bodies all the time. My brothers teased me about this, but I took my mom into her bedroom to show her that she saw colors too, but she told me she never had. I was in big pause mode, age twelve … my world just got rocked. I felt a bit odd and freakish and I left the dinner table stunned, trying to imagine a world without seeing these colors around other people's bodies. I wondered which of my friends saw these colors and which didn't.

My mom, without my permission, called UCLA to say she

had a daughter who saw auras. I guess my mom told our family friends, Aron Abrahamsen (a past-life reader who was young and practiced on our family, becoming famous for his gift) about me seeing auras. He advised my mom to call UCLA as they might be able to help her and me to understand more.

Apparently, because someone there knew Aron Abrahamsen, they gladly set up an appointment and we drove one and a half hours to UCLA. I went through some testing and saw the Kirlian photography camera. The photos did capture what I saw. They said they wanted to work with me. I was frightened that my normal way of seeing colors around people would be altered if I became a test subject, or that is what I told myself. I did not want to make a big deal about something that was normal to me, so I declined. My hunch now looking back is that my saying no helped me to keep myself invisible.

Reader:

- Most children have psychic awareness and they are okay if they have it or not. The key is to let children know they are okay being themselves and it's okay to be seen and be their true selves.

- Listen to what they experience. They might hear voices, see angels, auras, or see dead family members. It's all okay.

- They might see things and colors they cannot explain.*

- "What quantum physics teaches us is that everything we thought was physical is not physical." – Bruce H. Lipton, PhD

  *Links and book references provided as a source guide.

"I don't think there is any such thing as an ordinary mortal. Everybody has his own possibility of rapture in the experience of life. All he has to do is recognize it and then cultivate it and get going with it. I always feel uncomfortable when people speak about ordinary mortals because I've never met an ordinary man, woman, or child."

– Joseph Campbell

Dream at Age Four

I had this dream several times as a young girl and throughout my life.

A woman with short blonde hair and wearing big Hollywood sunglasses picks me up in a 1950s pink Cadillac convertible. A few other people are in the car and they make room for me. We are in Los Angeles and driving toward the desert. There are blue skies and the air is dry and warm. The blonde, as she is driving, asks me if I know what I am looking for and I say yes. She smiles and says good. We keep driving. We are out in the middle of nowhere in the desert going east.

I suddenly ask the woman driving to stop the car. She pulls off the road. I say, "I know this is where it is." I walk to the yellow painted line in the middle of the road and peel back the yellow line. It lifts up easily. I keep peeling it back, then finally I see a golden key. I know this is what I need, and it is my key. I take it back to the folks waiting for me in the pink car. They are happy I found my key and we continue driving down the freeway.

Reader:

- Can you recall a recurring dream from your childhood?

- Is your dream asking you to pay attention?

- Can you help and teach your children to learn and listen to their dreams?

- What if dreams are more important than you think?

- What if dreams are trying to guide and help you in your daily life?

"I honor health as the first muse, and sleep as the condition of health. Sleep benefits mainly by the sound health it produces; incidentally also by dreams, into whose farrago a divine lesson is sometimes slipped."

– Ralph Waldo Emerson, Letters and Social Aims

Little Flying Saucer

Age Ten

We are having a BBQ in our backyard. My whole family is there. I see a flying saucer way out in the distance. I am mesmerized by the color of the blue lights on this little shiny spaceship. My whole family looks up at the flying saucer. Suddenly in the blink of an eye the spaceship jumps closer to us. We all are not talking. We are silent and watch. Then it shifts again directly over our heads and closer to us. I am still only seeing the blue lights and now how huge this spaceship is, with my head tilted back. We are standing underneath, and it is huge.

We live near Vandenberg Air Force Base on the Central California Coast and often watch missiles shooting off into the sky like big firecrackers on a regular basis.

This is different.

I am feeling very calm, and time freezes.

I often forget completely about this experience. Other days out of the blue, I remember it vividly. My mom has the exact same memory as mine about this. My siblings do not recall it at all.

Reader:

- Are big questions okay to ask?

- Have you ever seen a flying saucer and/or an alien or something that seemed extraordinary?

- Why are we taught, and why do we teach children, not to be open to other living beings in this huge cosmic universe?

- What if we teach children to see and experience with openness and wonder, and to see that our universe is full of endless possibilities?

- Do you recall a time when you felt in wonder? What if it's not only okay, but healthy to pause and experience wonder?

- How can you bring more wonder and openness into your life right now?

- How can you teach your children, or students that it's okay to be more open and explore new possibilities?

- "I find many adults are put off when young children pose scientific questions. Why is the moon round? Why is the grass green? What is a dream? How deep can you dig a hole? When is the world's birthday? Why do we have toes? Too many teachers and parents answer with irritation or ridicule, or quickly move on to something else: What did you expect the moon to be, square? Children soon recognize that somehow this kind of question annoys grown-ups. A few more experiences like it, and another child is lost to science. Why adults should pretend to omniscience before age six-year-olds, I can't for the life of me understand. What's wrong with admitting that we don't know something? Is our self-esteem so fragile?" – Carl Sagan, The Demon-Haunted World: Science as a Candle in the Dark.

"Then, looking beyond the Earth itself to the magnificence of the larger scene, there was a startling recognition that the nature of the universe was not as I had been taught. My understanding of the separate distinctness and the relative independence of movement of those cosmic bodies was shattered. There was an upwelling of fresh insight coupled with a feeling of ubiquitous harmony – a sense of interconnectedness with the celestial bodies surrounding our spacecraft. Particular scientific facts about stellar evolution took on new significance."

– Edgar D. Mitchell, *The Way of the Explorer*

Little Girl

Big Dyslexia

I always did things differently but did not know I was different until I went to school.

I saw numbers backwards and letters reversed.

I struggled with math but then could get straight A's in my chemistry classes.

Spelling was and is always difficult.

I was told in fifth or sixth grade I had a high IQ.

But then why did I not feel so smart?

When I learned in the early 1980s that I was dyslexic I loved learning I had a disability.

It was something tactile to me that made sense, finally, of why my brain worked very differently.

Later in the 1990s when the education world tried to soften dyslexia as a learning difference I would not accept it, as to me it was and is more than a learning difference…. I understand the need to make it more acceptable for other kids, but for me it helped to accept my dyslexia as a handicap.

I often wondered, and still ponder, if because my brain is different, it developed more psychic abilities in order to help me live and survive in this world. This would require much research, but I would not be surprised if there is a correlation.

Reader:

- Are you dyslexic? Are your kids dyslexic?

- Be patient with yourself and with your children. Know that possibly if you are dyslexic you also might have psychic abilities or extrasensory awareness.

- Please see my referral list at the back of the book for further help.

"You can teach a student a lesson for a day; but if you can teach him to learn by creating curiosity, he will continue the learning process as long as he lives."

– Clay P. Bedford

Little Girl

Getting Older

Connecting the Dots ... Looking Back. Looking Now.

Somewhere in my life I began to want to help demonstrate that children are born with a knowing, an innate wisdom. As I grew older and had my little friend Brett across the street, he confirmed this to me.

He also knew where he came from before being born. He knew that I knew too, and talked about it with me. I interviewed him, and I was only twelve. Looking back now, that was abnormal, but since my mom was open to these things, it was normal to me. I had world-renowned or to-be-renowned practitioners doing "life readings" for me, introducing me to the Akashic records when I was about nine years old. This was not weird to me. It seemed normal within our home. I found everything these practitioners told me to be true within my little big world.

I had my blonde Hollywood woman in a 1950s pink Cadillac convertible driving down the freeway heading toward the desert and me finding the golden key dream on and off. It gave me a sense that I was still on the right path over the years of: colleges, marriages, having a son, living in Baja, trips abroad, traveling internationally interviewing kids about "Where do we come from? Why are we here? Do you see angels? God? Death? Rebirth?" Trying to demonstrate children's wisdom. Trying to demonstrate that children's voices should be heard; they should have a voice.

At one point long ago when I was doing research at UC Berkeley, I had all of my interview tapes with me in a box that I was going to drop off to have transcribed. Most interviews in this book were the first to get translated and transcribed over 40 years ago. That day at Berkeley, my car was broken into and my stereo and box of tapes were taken. This was devastating for me and put me on a big pause. I had forgotten that these few tapes had been transcribed. It was a few years later that I discovered my translated interviews. This was in the late 1980s when I came across a box with the interviews in it.

The interviews in this book demonstrate kids' sense of a deep universal knowing and soul knowing, just like mine. It has been such a hard, long, magical journey. When I recently learned that Brett was still the Brett that I interviewed over five decades ago, I wept.

May these next interviews open unknown spaces within your heart and mind, elevating your experience of childhood. May you read and listen to the children's words and ponder the possibilities.

"Dreams are nocturnal flowers, blooming when the sun has strayed far enough that we can see clearly."

– Terri Guillemets

Part Two: Interviews – Where Do We Come From?

"I love being a mother. I feel connected to a whole in bringing a life into this world. My grandfather died when my oldest daughter was two. I was just barely pregnant. We were driving in the car and I was very sad. My daughter asked, 'are you sad because grandpa is dead?' and I replied that I was sad for me and sad for my grandmother that he was gone. And she said to me, 'don't worry mommy, he will come back as a baby.' I almost drove off the road. Here I was pregnant with my second baby and she said this unprovoked. I do not believe in reincarnation or God per se and I'm very up in the air about my beliefs in general, but that really gave me pause."

– Interview of Cynthia by Wynn McClenahan Burkett, Life after Baby

Brett, age 4, USA

EMMA: Where do you come from?

BRETT: From the spirit house.

EMMA: What is the spirit house?

BRETT: A place where we wait to be born.

EMMA: What does it look like?

BRETT: You only see eyes, the rest you cannot see. Then when we get here, we know each other, because the eyes are the same.

EMMA: Why do the eyes stay the same?

BRETT: So we will remember each other. That's how I remember your eyes.

EMMA: My eyes?

BRETT: Yes, they are the same. That's why they look old.

EMMA: How come I don't remember the spirit house?

BRETT: Because you left the spirit house first. You are more away from it, because you are older.

EMMA: What else do you remember?

BRETT: There are always some eyes that stay forever in the spirit house. They watch over the other eyes, as they come and go.

45

EMMA: Why do they watch over the eyes?

BRETT: Because the spirit house can't get crowded. Otherwise everything gets in a big mess.

EMMA: Are you sure you remember my eyes?

BRETT: Yes. Maybe we will meet again in the spirit house and play together.

"No one has yet realized the Wealth and Sympathy, the Kindness, and Generosity hidden in the Soul of the child. The effort of every true education should be to unlock that treasure."

– Emma Goldman

Eddie, age 6, Mexico

EMMA: Where do you come from?

EDDIE: From the stomach.

EMMA: What was it like in the stomach?

EDDIE: I knocked for a long time on mama's stomach.

EMMA: Why did you knock?

EDDIE: Because I wanted to get out.

EMMA: How long did you knock?

EDDIE: As long as it took to cut the stomach.

EMMA: Did your mama hear the knocking?

EDDIE: No!

EMMA: What happened before you knocked?

EDDIE: I was lying very still.

"Grown men can learn from little children, for the hearts of little children are pure. Therefore, the Great Spirit may show to them many things which older people miss."

– Black Elk

Emmette, age 6, Germany

EMMA: Where do you come from?

EMMETTE: From the stomach. It was nice. It was nice to kick. I was very small.

EMMA: Where were you before the stomach?

EMMETTE: With God. It was also nice.

EMMA: Were there others with you, while you were with God?

EMMETTE: Yes, they were beautiful. They didn't look like me, they had black eyes.

"Overall, children don't realize the magic that can live inside their own heads. Better even than any movie."

– Eckhart Tolle

Whittney, age 6, USA

EMMA: Where does the sky come from?

WHITTNEY: The clouds.

EMMA: Where do the clouds come from?

WHITTNEY: From God.

EMMA: Where does God come from?

WHITTNEY: You can't see God that much....

EMMA: Can you see God a little bit?

WHITTNEY: No.

EMMA: What is God like?

WHITTNEY: A person who lives in the clouds.

EMMA: What does God do in the clouds?

WHITTNEY: He can see people and he can be around people.

EMMA: What does he do?

WHITTNEY: I just told you!

EMMA: Where does God come from?

WHITTNEY: [*screaming*] The sky!

EMMA: Where do you come from?

WHITTNEY: San Francisco

EMMA: Where were you before you were in San Francisco?

WHITTNEY: You mean before I was born?

EMMA: Yes, where did you come from?

WHITTNEY: In my mom's stomach.

EMMA: What was it like in there?

WHITTNEY: Blood in there. My mom says I could swim in the blood.

EMMA: If you could remember, what did it feel like in there?

WHITTNEY: It felt like nothing.

EMMA: Did it feel like anything else?

WHITTNEY: It felt like kicking. In the daytime I slept, and, in the night, I was awake.

EMMA: Could you hear inside your mom's tummy?

WHITTNEY: Yep! [*giggling*]

EMMA: What did you hear?

WHITTNEY: Her talking.

EMMA: What did mom say?

WHITTNEY: [*a big smile*] She was talking to my dad. She said the F word.

EMMA: Where were you before your mom's tummy?

WHITTNEY: With a sperm and an egg. But guess what? My cousin had a miscarriage.

EMMA: What happens to the baby when there is a miscarriage?

WHITTNEY: They die in the stomach.

EMMA: What happens next to them?

WHITTNEY: Up to heaven. [*pointing up*]

EMMA: What is that like?

WHITTNEY: You dream that you are going to heaven first. Then you go up to heaven.

EMMA: What's heaven like?

WHITTNEY: A lot of people. My dad's dad, Julius. My dad's mom, Grace. Then there is Dick. My babysitter's brother.

EMMA: Are you going there?

WHITTNEY: Yep.

EMMA: What does it look like?

WHITTNEY: First of all, there's brown stuff on the earth and little signs that stick up. The signs say who died. They put roses on them. But they don't see them, because they are in heaven.

EMMA: Who's in heaven?

WHITTNEY: The dead people.

EMMA: Do the dead people ever come back to earth?

WHITTNEY: Nope.

EMMA: What do they do?

WHITTNEY: They stay in heaven for a bit, then they float back
            down to San Francisco. Once you die, you go to
            heaven. But if you ever need to go to heaven before
            you die, you can if you need to. [*squinting her
            eyes*]. You dream in your mind but you only do this
            if you need to go badly!

EMMA: Do you do this?

WHITTNEY: Yep, if I really want to go, I go in my dreams.

EMMA: When do you go?

WHITTNEY: Yep, I did it a few days ago. You can do it too.

EMMA: How?

WHITTNEY: Close your eyes, then dream you are floating up to
            the heaven. Then you see dead people and God.

EMMA: What does God look like?

WHITTNEY: You already asked me that question.

EMMA: I know.

WHITTNEY: He's white. [*screaming*] So you can dream and go
          to heaven in the middle of the night, when it's dark!

*"Children are the hands by which we take hold
of heaven."*

– Henry Ward Beecher

Maxine, age 10, USA

EMMA: Any answer is correct. So, where do you think you come from?

MAXINE: Germany.

EMMA: And before that?

MAXINE: Ahhh. Africa.

EMMA: And before that?

MAXINE: The big, um....

EMMA: The big what?

MAXINE: The big, um, the island, the big island....

EMMA: Well that's okay, so big island?

MAXINE: Yeah.

EMMA: Okay and before that? Before you were on a big island?

MAXINE: Um, I don't know.

EMMA: So, if you knew. If you had the answers....

MAXINE: Oh, well....

EMMA: Like a fantasy, you know.... Or if you don't want to say "you," you could say, or where does the very first baby come from? That's another way to look at it. You can think about it. It's a big question.

MAXINE: It's … I think … I know they come from chimpanzees and I don't know how chimpanzees are made.

EMMA: So, where did the very first chimpanzees come
from?

MAXINE: Fishes.

EMMA: And so, where did the very first fishes come from?

MAXINE: Plants.

EMMA: The very first plants?

MAXINE: Big bang.

EMMA: Okay. And where did the very first big bang come
from?

MAXINE: Gas and dust and sun and the universe.

EMMA: Okay, and so do you think there was more than one
universe?

MAXINE: Yeah.

EMMA: Do you have any idea of why we are here? Like,
why are people on Earth?

MAXINE: No. I don't know.

EMMA: But if you knew? What if you had a unicorn who
            came down and said, "Okay, Maxine, you have all
            the answers."

MAXINE: Well, I just, maybe, like … we're here to discover
            stuff. And, to … I think we're here to inhabit the
            earth and keep it pristine, but that's not happening.

EMMA: Yeah, which is kind of sad. So, say that again: we
            are here to inhabit the earth?

MAXINE: And keep it pristine, but we're not doing that.

EMMA: Do you think there are ways we could do that? Be-
            cause, I agree with you.

MAXINE: There probably is, but we would have to, like, stop
            everything.

EMMA: Mmm hmmm. As we are doing….

MAXINE: Yeah.

EMMA: Yeah, so let's imagine we stop doing everything,
            then what could we do to make it pristine again?

MAXINE: Everyone … I mean, I guess like, everybody from
            every town could clean the air, some houses, pick
            up all the trash, stop using their cars.

EMMA: Just get to work.

MAXINE: Yeah. Not use so much energy.

EMMA: Mmm hmm. Everyone have solar. Live differently.

MAXINE: Live green.

EMMA: Live green. I just wonder how we're going to moti-
            vate people to do that. How do you think people,
            you know…. I think you have some answers there!
            Because, you seem like you know.

MAXINE: Um, I think we need to get rid of all the oil produc-
            ers and the plastic manufacturers, and the, um, other
            things.

EMMA: Everything….

MAXINE: The car producers. And just forget about all of that.
            It's going to be hard because we are living in an age
            where everything is polluting the earth.

"The world is a complicated place, but if you believe in love, unicorns and yourself, you will survive."

– Maxine, El Granada, CA

Emma, age 5, USA

EMMA: Where does the sun come from?

Little Emma: The clouds.

EMMA: Where do the clouds come from?

Little Emma: The rain.

EMMA: Where do you come from?

Little Emma: My mommy's tummy.

EMMA: What was it like in there?

Little Emma: Rolling around and all squeezed up like an egg roll.

EMMA: How did it feel?

Little Emma: Tight!

EMMA Did you want out?

Little Emma: Probably. Out! Out! Out!

EMMA Could you hear anything?

Little Emma: Her echo.

EMMA: What did her echo sound like?

Little Emma: Like her voice, but different. I was inside instead of out. It sounded like she was really far away, but she wasn't ... she was right there.

EMMA: Can you remember what your mommy said?

Little Emma: "I want my baby to come out now!" Then she had me.

EMMA: What else was it like?

Little Emma: When she was under the covers it was better because I was warmer.

EMMA: Could you see anything while you were inside your mommy's tummy?

Little Emma: Yep, but it was very dark and round … I don't know.

EMMA: Did you feel anything?

Little Emma: Kind of alone.

EMMA: What did it feel like to be alone?

Little Emma: Like when I sleep alone now.

EMMA: Can you remember further back?

Little Emma: (laughter) Further? You mean before I was in my mom's stomach?

EMMA: Yes, what was that like?

Little Emma: Nowhere, just plain air.

EMMA: What's air like?

Little Emma: Cold but you can't see it.

EMMA: Could I see you?

Little Emma: Nope. I wasn't made yet.

EMMA: Were you alone in the air?

Little Emma: Nope, others were with me.

EMMA: What did you do with the others?

Little Emma: We played invisible and made artwork.

EMMA: Was everything invisible?

Little Emma: Yep, no one could see it except me.

EMMA: How come just you?

Little Emma: Because I was drawing in the air. (Drawing with finger in the air)

EMMA: Do you have a body in the air?

Little Emma: Everything is invisible in the air.

EMMA: How did you get from the air to here?

Little Emma: We saw these people on the block, then we picked who we wanted to be with.

EMMA: How did you pick your mom?

Little Emma: I was first. I wanted her to be my mom. She had nice clothes on. She was very nice. Then we would be able to see each other.

EMMA: How would she see you?

Little Emma: When I'm ready to be with her I don't have the power to be invisible anymore.

EMMA   How do you lose it?

Little Emma: I share it with the kids before I'm ready to go to my mom.

EMMA: So, you gave it to them?

Little Emma: Yes, so they could use it. I ran out of my power because I shared it too much.

EMMA: Did you like losing your power?

Little Emma: Yep, because I was sharing it with others.

EMMA: So, then what happened?

Little Emma: When I was done sharing, I had no more power to be invisible, then I came to my mom.

EMMA: Did you like being invisible?

Little Emma: [*laughing*] Yes, I loved it.

EMMA: Will you be invisible again?

Little Emma: When I go to the magic mirror and say, "Mirror, please give me some magic power."

EMMA: What happens when you die?

Little Emma: Get burned up. Then up to heaven.

EMMA: What's heaven like?

Little Emma: Up in the air, invisible, then people throw flowers out. I can see the flowers because I'm already in heaven.

EMMA: Do you like it in heaven?

Little Emma: I like it in heaven because there are others with me in heaven. More people that died before me.

EMMA: Who would be there?

Little Emma: A grown-up friend.

EMMA: How come they would be there?

Little Emma: They would be waiting for me. They would say, "Haven't I seen you before?"

EMMA: What would you say?

Little Emma: I'd say, "I think I've seen you."

EMMA: Then what would happen?

Little Emma: They take me to a dead playground. It's old and rusty but I don't care, because at least it's a playground. It's an invisible playground. It's part visible and part invisible. All of the swings are invisible and the slides are visible.

EMMA: How would you stop wars?

Little Emma: I'd get this big thing that was invisible. I'd talk into
              it and tell everybody that was fighting to please stop
              fighting. Because there will be less people if we
              keep killing.

EMMA: Why would you need an invisible thing to say this
              to them?

Little Emma: Because then they couldn't fight with me. They
              wouldn't know where the thoughts to stop fighting
              were coming from, so they'd have nothing to fight
              against. So, they would think it was their thoughts
              and not mine. If I was invisible I could get away if
              they did try to fight me, but they would still hear the
              words, "Don't fight please".

"I was certainly no more than six or seven when I began to feel myself drawn by Matter, or more exactly by something that shone, at the heart of matter. I had caught the usual child religion from my mom, but this secret preoccupation was an entirely separate kind of 'worship'; it was the worship of Iron."

– Teilhard de Chardin

Goshav, age 12, Russia

EMMA: I'd like you to tell me something about how your life got started.

GOSHAV: My mother gave birth to me.

EMMA: Where were you before you were born?

GOSHAV: I think that my soul used to belong to another man, but after the death of that man, it was incarnated into me, now it is my soul.

EMMA: Tell me more about what the soul is like.

GOSHAV: The soul is something that a human being can't see at all. It is invisible to man.

EMMA: What else can you tell me about it?

GOSHAV: After the death of a human being, the soul flies into the cosmos, and passes through some planet. While it is passing through this planet, it gets rid of all thoughts, features, knowledge and character of this particular person, then it flies back to earth. It then finds a body in which it incarnates, but it will be a pure soul, and gradually, it starts acquiring the features to make it typical for that person.

EMMA: What is it like when the soul is in the pure state?

GOSHAV: I believe the soul has the form of a human body, but you can't see it at all. Maybe some machines might see this matter, but it is not visible to human beings.

EMMA: How did the soul get started, and how was it born, or how did it start?

GOSHAV: The soul appears at the same time as the creature, whether it is a human being or an animal. Animal souls are much simpler.

EMMA: How did the soul begin?

GOSHAV: I believe in the science aspect, that first the galaxy appeared, then the globe, then some animals. From the animals, the human beings started. The soul was always inside the living creatures.

EMMA: How did the cosmos get started?

GOSHAV: It is a very difficult question. No one can really give an answer, but I believe that it is the will of nature which is the most powerful and which might do everything.

EMMA: How do you know these things?

GOSHAV: Actually, I have gotten the information from different sources. Mother and Father have told me some things, I have read some things, and even from songs. I have given it some thought and I came up with the system which appeals to me the most.

EMMA: Do you feel your soul or is it just an idea to you?

GOSHAV: I do feel the soul inside of me, and I feel that the soul is me. It is something inside of me and it is the features of my character. I feel the character and the soul are the same things.

EMMA: Does your father talk about the soul?

GOSHAV: Well, my father didn't talk specifically about this particular subject. He told me fragments from different talks about some pictures and some books. I gathered the information and pondered it, and now I feel that I have my system, something that I believe in very much.

"After a while, the middle-aged person who lives in her head begins to talk to her soul, the kid."

– Anne Lamott

Dagney, age 9, USA

EMMA: Where does the sun come from?

DAGNEY: Oh god, that's a hard question. Can I say what it is made out of?

EMMA: Yes, anything you say is okay.

DAGNEY: Light.

EMMA: Where does light come from?

DAGNEY: Electricity.

EMMA: Where does electricity come from?

DAGNEY: I'm not sure.

EMMA: Just imagine; anything you say is okay.

DAGNEY: Oh, god.

EMMA: Where do you come from?

DAGNEY: [*laughing*] Oh no, earth still.

EMMA: Before you were a tiny baby, where did you come from?

DAGNEY: [*laughing*] It was fun. I could kick. I could actually do whatever I wanted, instead of being bossed around. It was fun.

EMMA: Did you want to come out or did you want to stay in

there?

DAGNEY: Well usually babies cry when they want to come out. I don't think I wanted to come out.

EMMA: Why?

DAGNEY: Because it was nice.

EMMA: Where were you before mom's tummy?

DAGNEY: I could have been born any place. I think I was in Paris.

EMMA: Where were you before Paris?

DAGNEY: On another planet.

EMMA: What did it look like?

DAGNEY: Orange and red lights.

EMMA: Where were you before the planet?

DAGNEY: Oh, god, that's a hard question. Maybe I saw another person, someone else. I might have been an animal.

EMMA: Before you were another person?

DAGNEY: [*laughing*] These are hard questions. I was rich.

EMMA: How did you get from the planet to mom's tummy?

DAGNEY: Well, maybe I died on the planet, came back to earth. It's like a new life.

EMMA: How did you come to your mom?

DAGNEY: I picked her.

EMMA: Would you ever like to go back to your planet?

DAGNEY: Yes, I'd like to try it out again.

EMMA: Can you go there now?

DAGNEY: Only in a spaceship.

EMMA: What happens when you die?

DAGNEY: I go to another life. I'm not sure. Maybe I wouldn't have another life.

EMMA: What would happen?

DAGNEY: I wouldn't exist. I might go to heaven.

EMMA: What's heaven like?

DAGNEY: It must be fun up there. I dream in the clouds and go on and on. It is soft and fun.

EMMA: Are you alone?

DAGNEY: No, I see my relatives that have died.

EMMA: Do you ever go beyond heaven?

DAGNEY: Maybe to the opposite. It is hard and rocky.

EMMA: Is earth a hard and rocky place?

DAGNEY: It's both. So, you can be comfortable if you want to.

76

Maybe write or play a board game.

EMMA: Is it hard in heaven?

DAGNEY: Nope, it's soft and you don't eat because you're dead. You don't waste your time eating in heaven. But sometimes you go to school in heaven.

EMMA: Is God there?

DAGNEY: Sometimes.

EMMA: Where is God if God's not in heaven?

DAGNEY: Might be somewhere else but close by.

EMMA: What does God look like?

DAGNEY: God can be a lady or a man.

EMMA: Do you ever see angels?

DAGNEY: Yes.

EMMA: What do they look like?

DAGNEY: Well, they have wings, wear a white uniform, curly blond hair.

EMMA: What color are their wings?

DAGNEY: White.

EMMA: Do you see them in heaven or here?

DAGNEY: Only when I dream. When I dream people don't talk, it's more like they are with me.

EMMA: What does it feel like to be with the angels?

DAGNEY: It feels really strong. Sometimes I think I am really there. It's a little freaky because sometimes I don't know if I can come back.

EMMA: Do you have a soul?

DAGNEY: Yes.

EMMA: Does it die?

DAGNEY: No.

EMMA: What happens to the soul when we die?

DAGNEY: It goes with us.

EMMA: To?

DAGNEY: Heaven or maybe to another planet.

EMMA: Where does God come from?

DAGNEY: God was born from a beam.

EMMA: Why are we here?

DAGNEY: God made up the rules. Monkeys started out.

EMMA: What is the purpose of being here?

DAGNEY: There's a reason but I don't know it.

EMMA: Why did you come?

DAGNEY: Just to try it out.

EMMA: Why do we have wars?

DAGNEY: People fight but there is no reason for it. People just need to talk.

EMMA: What could you do to stop the fighting and wars?

DAGNEY: It wouldn't work. No one would listen to a nine-year-old kid. They think they are right. But I'd destroy all of the weapons.

EMMA: Why do they want to fight?

DAGNEY: Well, maybe from the start they didn't want to live. So then to them it doesn't matter if they fight or kill because they really don't want to live. But they shouldn't make others die, just because they want to die. They can make the bomb because they want to die, and they don't consider others' right to live.

EMMA: What would happen if the world blew up?

DAGNEY: God would make another planet and beam us back down.

EMMA: How does God do that?

DAGNEY: God has power.

EMMA: Do we have power like that?

DAGNEY: Nope, no one has power like God.

EMMA: Does the soul ever come back?

DAGNEY: Yes, but it depends on where you want to come back to, another country, another planet or any place.

EMMA: Why would the soul come back?

DAGNEY: Well, if you thought your life was fun but you died too young, before you were ready to die, then you redo it and come back.

EMMA: Do you ever see people from the planet you were on?

DAGNEY: Yes, my friends and some teachers, but not my family.

EMMA: How do you recognize someone from another planet?

DAGNEY: You just know by remembering them.

EMMA: Did your parents teach you these thoughts?

DAGNEY: No, I just made them up as you asked the questions.

"Their questions must be taken seriously; if one can use such opportunities to instill in them a spiritual conception of life, allow them to feel greatness and beauty of the universe and the admirable order that characterizes it ... at the same time, one must observe and encourage all spontaneous manifestations of a spiritual nature such as higher aspirations, intuitions and illuminations that might arise in them."

– Dr. Assagioli

George, age 12, Russia

EMMA: Where does the sun come from?

GEORGE: It is difficult to answer this question. I have never
            given it a thought.

EMMA: How did you get started?

GEORGE: From my mother.

EMMA: Where were you before you got started?

GEORGE: In the cosmos.

EMMA: What was it like?

GEORGE: After my death, I flew to the cosmos, and I might
            have lived on another planet, then I returned back. I
            believe that I have lived many lives and this is what
            has happened.

EMMA: What is your soul like?

GEORGE: It has no definite form, like air. When I am in the
            cosmos, I am in this form, then when I come back
            to Earth, I choose a body and start living inside.

EMMA: What is that like on the other planet?

GEORGE: The soul just floats around the other planet during
            the intermediate time, then it comes back to Earth.

EMMA: Why does the soul come into a body?

GEORGE: The soul can't exist by itself, it has to come back to a body.

EMMA: Is there a reason?

GEORGE: It just should return back.

EMMA: How do you know these things? Did someone tell you these things?

GEORGE: I really don't know. When I was very small, I never thought of it. But when I did think of it, I felt that it was probably this way.

EMMA: How did your soul get started?

GEORGE: When the Earth started, it was all plants, then there were animals, then human beings. When human beings started, the soul was already part of them. A human being appeared from a monkey, both the body and the soul together.

EMMA: Do monkeys have a soul?

GEORGE: When the soul is flying to the cosmos, it has all the manners of the person it was part of, then it is something pure, and then it is reincarnated into a baby and gradually it obtains knowledge and grows.

EMMA: What is it like in that pure state?

GEORGE: In that pure state, it has all the knowledge and thoughts and features of a person, but it is also vacant.

EMMA: How did the cosmos get started?

GEORGE: It is very difficult to say. I feel like a computer center trying to say how it was all originated. My thoughts just flow away.

EMMA: What happens when your thoughts flow away?

GEORGE: I am looking at the sky, and the clouds, and the trees, but I can't concentrate my thoughts. Just now, or when you are asking me questions, I look out the window and it takes my attention, and I could be in another place.

"There is no single effort more radical in its potential for saving the world than a transformation of the way we raise our children."

– Marianne Williamson

Lori, age 11, China

EMMA: So, this is an imagination game. There's no wrong
          answers. Anything you say is fine. You're not being
          graded. I'm just putting that out there. So, where do
          you think the first mother came from?

LORI: Mary.

EMMA: Okay.

LORI: No, that's a lie.

EMMA: Well, what do you think? There's no....

LORI: Eve.

EMMA: And where do you think Eve came from?

LORI: God.

EMMA: Where did God come from?

LORI: [*laughing*] The universe.

EMMA: And where did the universe come from?

LORI: Imagination.

EMMA: Where did imagination come from?

LORI: The mind.

EMMA: Where did the mind come from?

LORI: Humans.

EMMA: And where did humans come from?

LORI: A person.

EMMA: Where does a person come from?

LORI: Um, God.

EMMA: And so, where do you come from?

LORI: Like, where am I from?

EMMA: It can be anything.

LORI: I want to be a cat.

EMMA: So, you want to be a cat? Do you think you ever were a cat?

LORI: Nope.

EMMA: But right now, you would like to be a cat.

LORI: Yep.

EMMA: That's cool. So what is it about being a cat that you like?

LORI: They are fuzzy, cute and they always land on their feet. So, when I fall off a twenty-story building, I might as well not fall on my face.

EMMA: Yes, so you can be safe. So when you were a little baby, where did you come from?

LORI: My mom.

EMMA: And, can you remember what it was like inside your mom?

LORI: [*squinting her eyes tightly shut and putting her index fingers up on her temples*] Black.

EMMA: What did it feel like? Black, and….

LORI: Ah, it felt like nothing.

EMMA: Did it have a feeling? Did nothing have a feeling?

LORI: Yeah, nothing had a feeling because I kind of don't remember.

EMMA: What about before you were in your mummy's tummy? Before you were in nothing? Where did you come from?

LORI: I was being created by God.

EMMA: What was that like?

LORI: I don't know.

EMMA: Well, if you knew?

LORI: I can make this up?

EMMA: You can totally make this up.

LORI: I was a cat.

EMMA: And what was that like, being a cat?

LORI: It was fun.

EMMA: And what about before you were a cat?

LORI: I was a kitten!

EMMA: And before you were a kitten?

LORI: I was not born.

EMMA: And before you weren't born?

LORI: I was nothing.

EMMA: And before you were nothing, what were you?

LORI: A ghost.

EMMA: And what was that like being a ghost?

LORI: Fun.

EMMA: So, being a ghost, could you see? Were you in ghost
            world or were you in this world? What was it like
            being a ghost?

LORI: I was ghosty.

EMMA: And what is ghosty like?

LORI: Fun to fly I guess.

EMMA: Ah. Did you have wings?

LORI: I could levitate.

EMMA: So you could just kind of instantaneously go….
           What was levitating like?

LORI: Flying without wings.

EMMA: Oh, nice.

LORI: [*starts singing and using floaty hand motions*] Like
           flying like a ghost. I don't know how to explain it.

EMMA: Well you just did. And before you were flying like a
           ghost?

LORI: Um, I was dust.

EMMA: Mmmm. And what was that like?

LORI: I had no feelings. Hmm.

EMMA: You didn't have them? Or did you have feelings?

LORI: Nope. I was dust.

EMMA: And before you were dust?

LORI: I was a star.

EMMA: What was that like being a star?

LORI: I just had to sit there until the moon came.

EMMA: And then what happened when the moon came?

LORI: [*singing*] I got to shine!

EMMA: Ah, nice. It feels like you remember that.

LORI:	I don't know.
EMMA:	No? Okay. And so what was that like – shining?
LORI:	It was fun. It was shiny. It was bright.
EMMA:	Do you ever connect to that place now? That shiny, bright place?
LORI:	Yeah, when I'm happy.
EMMA:	Uh-huh. So, it's similar?
LORI:	Yeah.
EMMA:	Let's imagine you have a magic wand and you can do anything–
LORI:	[interrupting] Turn into a cat.
EMMA:	Okay, we know that. You want to be a cat! Let's imagine you are a cat and you have a magic wand. How would you make the world a better place? What would you do?
LORI:	Stop war. Turn everybody into cats. I dunno. That just came to the top of my head … I just wanted to turn everybody into cats. Stop war. Make peace. Stop war, I guess. We just have to stop war. Oh yeah, stop pollution, stop war, stop global warming, stop the ice from melting which is basically global warming, but make it frozen again, take back the ice

age. Wait, why would I do that? Lori, think! Make the ice age possible. So, everyone knows what it feels like to be in the ice age.

EMMA: Say that again.

LORI: Everybody can feel like what it's like to be in the ice age.

EMMA: And what did that feel like?

LORI: Cold and a good experience, if you didn't die.

EMMA: That was a good thing. And so, if everything could be in the ice age again, how would that be good for everyone? How would that make things better?

LORI: Because we learn from our mistakes. Basically, it's like, from before war, it's like punishment to make everyone realize to stop war and help each other in the ice age, which will only last two days. Two 48-hour days. Every day will be 48 hours.

EMMA: And then what happens in those 48 hours?

LORI: You have to learn how to survive, because all of the animals die because they are frozen. Water freezes. You have to find shelter and stay alive. Oh, yeah, and go to the mall before everything freezes. To buy winter clothes.

92

EMMA: To take with you.

LORI: In summer.

EMMA: In summer. Okay. And so, right now, do you have any sense, at your age, of how you are going to help the world become a better place?

LORI: I was always thinking of making a charity or building a school, but I was thinking that would be a lot of money. So maybe, like, write a book.

EMMA: Maybe all of them. So, you'd like to write a book, have a charity and education? Wow that's really great. What else?

LORI: Yeah. And save endangered animals.

"It was 1952, and I am seven years old. On this particular day my parents and I are driving from the air force base of Nouasseur to the nearby city of Casablanca on a shopping expedition. It is a journey we have made many times before and I am sitting in the back seat of our car idly watching the scenery go by.

"All at once, I am filled with a feeling of energy coursing through my body and a sensation as if I'm expanding like a balloon. Before I can think about what is happening, I find myself somehow outside of my body but enveloping it. Looking down and in some fashion within at the same time, I see my physical form, my parents, tiny objects rapidly shrinking out of view. When they are gone, I am alone in an unbroken field of white light....

"I had a visual impression of the universe, a great wheel of stars and galaxies, suffused with the golden glow of millions of suns, floating in a sea of spirit. It was as if I were seeing as this presence saw, and for one instant we were one. In that instant, it was as if everything that existed, every atom, every stone, every world, every star, seeing creation not from some great distance but from the inside out, as if it were my own body and being."

– David Spangler, Emergence: The Rebirth of the Sacred

94

Mary, age 5, USA

EMMA: Where did the very first mother come from?

MARY: Nowhere.

EMMA: Nowhere?

MARY: A dinosaur laid an egg and it came and the baby came out and started walking and growing and growing and growing and then there was a mommy.

EMMA: Came from a dinosaur egg? Where did the dinosaur come from?

MARY: Everywhere.

EMMA: How did it do that?

MARY: It was all over the world, every single world. And then that person just *builded* a world and killed the dinosaurs and *builded* a world.

EMMA: Who killed the dinosaur?

MARY: The baby that was there had a gun.

EMMA: The baby that was in the egg?

MARY: Yeah, no, she *growed* up to be a mother and laid an egg and got a gun. And then she wasn't anything else but she was still a mother and she shot all of the dinosaurs and made a city.

"Where you really come from.
No matter how much worldly success you have
achieved,
way down in your bones you know that there is
much more to you than you've shown so far.
Like so many of us, you feel a deep yearning
to bring something vital, something uniquely
yours to the suffering world.
No amount of outward achievement, no amount
of fame, kudos or accolades can fill this yearning
to transcend your empty and separate sense of
'me'
and deliver to our world what you came here to
give.
You've had glimpses of a shimmering reality
behind our fractured and suffering world.
A golden honey colored realm of pure peace,
absolute acceptance, pure love.
It's where you really come from.
It's who you really are.
The door to that sacred reality opens inward.
It can be found in only one place;
The Present Moment."

– Neal Rogin, Delightment

Sheila, age 10, Russia

EMMA: Where do you come from?

SHEILA: I was given birth by my mother, but people in general came from monkeys.

EMMA: What was it like before you were born?

SHEILA: It was the last century.

EMMA: What was that like?

SHEILA: Well, as far as I know, if you are a human being, you can't be reincarnated as an animal, so in the last century, I must have been a human being.

EMMA: What kind of human being were you?

SHEILA: I don't know, because people don't know what kind of persons they were in their last bodies. Maybe a machine would know.

EMMA: What kind of machine?

SHEILA: I don't know. I just suppose there must be one that knows.

EMMA: What is it like, the time in between reincarnations?

SHEILA: In the last century. I was a human being, and then in between, maybe I was an insect, like a butterfly, because their life is so short, and then another reincarnation would happen. I didn't read this, I think it might be so.

EMMA: If you got into a rocket ship and went into space for a very long time, then where would you be?

SHEILA: Another planet.

EMMA: What if you went past the planet?

SHEILA: There is no limit to the cosmos, there will always be more planets.

EMMA: What if you were to go down? What would you find?

SHEILA: It is rock, and if you go through completely, you will find yourself on the other side of the Earth.

EMMA: How did the cosmos begin?

SHEILA: I don't know.

EMMA: When you become a person did you want to become a person?

SHEILA: Yes, because it is the best life you can have.

EMMA: Why? What is the best about it?

SHEILA: Humans are the strongest, and it is better to be strong than weak. If you look at animals, like a lion, they have to work very hard to get their food, but we don't have such worries. We can enjoy life.

EMMA: What will happen after you die?

SHEILA: Death is a rest from life. While you live, you have short rests, but death is a never-ending rest. After that, I would start living again.

EMMA: How did life, animals, and people get started?

SHEILA: It might have started from another planet, but there were a lot of forests and water, but there were no people.

EMMA: Then what happened?

SHEILA: The Earth came from a piece of another planet. Then gradually, different things came to be. There was a process, first monkeys, then people.

"A child can ask a thousand questions that the wisest man cannot answer."

– Jacob Abbott

Harry, age 8, China

EMMA: Who were you before you were here?

HARRY: Just a thought.

EMMA: And what about before you were a thought?

HARRY: Undiscovered thought. *Unthought* of thought. A
            thought that hasn't been thought of yet.

EMMA: Would it have a feeling? Are there feelings there?
            Or is a thought just a thought? How is it?

HARRY: I dunno. It's just a thought.

EMMA: Are there any colors in thoughts?

HARRY: In my head?

EMMA: Yes.

HARRY: I dunno. If it's an angry thought you know, red's
            usually associated with anger. So….

EMMA: And what if it's a thought before you were born?
            What would that color be?

HARRY: [*laughing*] Oh god, I dunno.

EMMA: [*laughing, too*] What if you knew?

HARRY: Green. Queasy green.

EMMA: Okay, if you had a magic wand and you could do
            anything with the wand to create world peace, what
            would you do?

HARRY: Anything to create world peace?

EMMA: Yes.

HARRY: Well right now there's a war on terrorism, right?
            Yeah, I'd use my magical wand to stop that. Um, I
            know there is crime and stuff in the world, lots of
            … well, that's the thing, the world has so many
            problems. Yeah, world peace is one big one. But
            there is poverty. Climate change. So, yeah, I dunno.
            Use my magic wand … obtain world peace, stop
            everyone from fighting. Well most people fight be-
            cause, I dunno, because they are greedy and they
            want money and they want power over other peo-
            ple, I dunno, religion maybe. In different parts of
            the world.

EMMA: So, would you get rid of religion? Or would you get
            rid of greed?

HARRY: Um, I dunno, greed seems like it's a part of human
            nature, you know. Kings and queens from hundreds
            of years ago were greedy, they killed their own kin
            just to have the power. I guess if you could get rid

of greed, that would be much better. Humans would just, if they were content, they had contentment, you know, you have something that you're content with, you're fine with it, you don't need more. No need to want more. Selfishness. Not wanting to share, I guess. I don't know. That's a tough one.

EMMA: When you smile, you know something. What do you know when you smile?

HARRY: Um, religion. How do I say this? Um. Jesus created the world. God created the world. I feel like in every religion it's just explanation of why things are. And then there are people who don't have religion, they have science, I guess. But yeah, in every religion I think maybe they were just made to explain why everything is. You know, who created the sun, the sky, you know and…. The Vikings, they had all of these gods and they had all of these realms and everything, and they just explained why things are. What things do. Why they do what they do. Humans didn't have an explanation for it, so they just made one up. And then other people believed them and … [*shrugging his shoulders*]

EMMA: And then they fight over them.

HARRY: Yeah. My idea's right. Yours is wrong. My idea should be the only idea. That's right. I dunno, and then they just fight.

EMMA: So, you would get rid of all of that with your magic wand?

HARRY: Yeah, kind of.

EMMA: What would you do?

HARRY: Well, now humans are smarter, I guess. We at least have an idea. We know what most things are. Now, we know that there isn't a mill at the bottom of the ocean grinding salt out, because like, I dunno, like, I think in Europe that was a legend that there was a mill and that's why the water is salty, but now we actually have a scientific explanation for why things are. Um, I guess, I would use my magic wand, then … I dunno. It's tough.

EMMA: It is tough. You're doing great.

HARRY: Yeah, I guess if everyone's arguing about ideas. My idea's wrong. Yours is right. Therefore, yeah, I guess if you could get rid of all that, that would be better.

EMMA: What if you knew? Do you have a sense of what you want to do to help the world?

HARRY: Like if I became a humanitarian?

EMMA: Maybe. I mean, it sounds like you already are.

HARRY: Wait, could you rephrase that?

EMMA: So, if you knew what you wanted to do to help the world, and you could do it, what would you be doing?

HARRY: Well, if I knew what I had to do and I knew how to do it? My magic wand is becoming useful. What do I want to do? Solve climate change obviously. Solve greed, yeah, selfishness. All the wars and all the fighting and everything. I dunno. We waste resources on all these wars. Um, so yeah, world peace? To solve that? I dunno. How do you solve world peace without a magic wand? You get the two sides to talk with each other.

EMMA: Do you think that's part of the reason why you were born? To help with this maybe?

HARRY: Maybe.

EMMA: Do you have any sense why you were born?

HARRY: Because, um, I have no clue.

EMMA: Well, if you knew?

HARRY: If I did know why I was born, if I knew what I was
            made to do and I did whatever I was made to do,
            wouldn't that then make my life meaningless? Be-
            cause I've already accomplished what I was meant
            to do?

EMMA: But maybe there would be something else after that
            you were supposed to do.

HARRY: Let's say I was made to be the first person on Mars.
            Once I get on Mars then…. How do I get on Mars?
            Become a fighter pilot. Get selected by NASA. Go
            to Mars.

EMMA: Do you want to do that? Is that something you want
            to do?

HARRY: Yeah. I like space. It would be pretty cool to be the
            first person on Mars.

EMMA: Is there anything you could do to make it a better
            place on Mars so we don't make mistakes?

HARRY: [*laughing*] Make it a better place on Mars?

EMMA: Yes, so we don't have the same mistakes we have
            here.

HARRY: Oh, yeah, I can see what you mean. Maybe … oh no, if humans live on Mars, obviously we are going to need a lot of food and water, and if one person has a lot of food and water and another person doesn't, and they are being selfish, um, I dunno....

EMMA: It's a lot to think about, but I think you have a sense of it.

HARRY: Um, if people lived on Mars, world peace hopefully. Hopefully no one would fight each other on Mars. They know that if they did, something bad probably would come out of it. World peace? Climate? I dunno. How could there be climate change on Mars?

EMMA: I don't know. How did we get climate change here?

HARRY: Fossil fuels. Oil.

EMMA: Right, so we don't want to go there and do the same thing, right?

HARRY: There's no atmosphere on Mars.

EMMA: That's true.

HARRY: So therefore, there can't be climate change, I guess. Maybe.

EMMA: Maybe. I don't know. Something to think about.

HARRY: Yeah. I guess it would be nice if people didn't fight
           each other. If people didn't fight each other on
           Mars, hopefully, we could spread out to the planets
           without killing each other.

EMMA: That seems pretty major for you.

HARRY: Yes!

"Love is what we are born with. Fear is what we learn. The spiritual journey is the unlearning of fear and prejudices and the acceptance of love back in our hearts. Love is the essential reality and our purpose on earth. To be consciously aware of it, to experience love in ourselves and others, is the meaning of life. Meaning does not lie in things. Meaning lies in us."

– Marianne Williamson

Johauna, age 11, Switzerland

EMMA: Where does the moon come from?

JOHAUNA: From the universe as a part of another star.

EMMA: Where does the other star come from?

JOHAUNA: From the atmosphere.

EMMA: Where does the atmosphere come from?

JOHAUNA: I can't really explain that.

EMMA: Where do you come from?

JOHAUNA: From Baden Writtenberg, then we moved several times.

EMMA: Where were you before that?

JOHAUNA: I was nothing, only air.

EMMA: How was it to be air?

JOHAUNA: I floated around, I didn't think of anything. It was dark.

EMMA: How was it before you were air?

JOHAUNA: I was nothing.

EMMA: How did you get from air to here?

JOHAUNA: Through my parents.

110

EMMA: Why did you leave the air?

JOHAUNA: Because I found my parents when they wanted chil-
            dren.

EMMA: Why did you come into this life?

JOHAUNA: Because mankind would be extinguished if there
            were no more children.

EMMA: Why do we need mankind?

JOHAUNA: Without people everything would be nothingness.

EMMA: Why did you leave the air?

JOHAUNA: Because life is enjoyable.

EMMA: Will you ever return to the air?

JOHAUNA: Yes, I will be a spirit and live in the atmosphere.

EMMA: Are there others in the air with you?

JOHAUNA: Only others like me. The air is dark.

EMMA: How long do you stay in the air?

JOHAUNA: I don't know, maybe life is a cycle from air to life
            and back to air.

EMMA: Is there a purpose to this cycle?

JOHAUNA: Yes, because there will always be more opportuni-
            ties to experience more beauty.

"He opened the geography to study the lesson; but he could not learn the names of places in America. Still they were all different places, that had different names. They were all in different countries and the different countries were in different continents and the continents were in the world and the world was in the universe.

"He turned to the fly leaf of the geography and what he had written there; himself, his name, and where he was.

Stephen Dedalus

Class of Elements

Clongowes Wood College

Sallins

County Kildare

Ireland

Europe

The World

The Universe

"He read the verses backwards but then they were not poetry. Then he read the fly leaf from bottom to the top till he came to his own name. That was he and he read the page again.

"What was after universe? Nothing. Was there anything round the universe to show where it stopped before the nothing place began? It could not be a wall but there could be a thin, thin line around everything. It was very big to think about everything, and everywhere. Only God could do that. He tried to think what a big thought that

must be but he could think only of God. God was God's name, just as his name was Stephen. Dieu was French for God and that was God's name too; and when anyone prayed to God and said Dieu then God knew at once that it was a French person that was praying. But though there were different names for God, in all the different languages in the world and God understood what all the people who prayed said in their different languages still God remained always the same God and God's real name was God. It made him very tired to think that way. It made him feel his head was very big."

– James Joyce, A Portrait of the Artist as a Young Man

Jill, age 11, USA

EMMA: Where were you before you were a baby?

JILL: In my mom's stomach.

EMMA: What was it like?

JILL: I don't know.

EMMA: If you could remember.

JILL: It was dark and warm.

EMMA: Did you like being there?

JILL: Yes.

EMMA: What did you like about it?

JILL: I liked being warm in my mom's stomach.

EMMA: Did you want to be born?

JILL: Yes.

EMMA: How come?

JILL: Because I wanted to see what it was like on the outside of my mom's stomach.

EMMA: When you were in your mom's stomach, did you know you were in her stomach?

JILL: No!

EMMA: Where did you think you were?

JILL: In a dark cave.

EMMA: Did you know there was a way out?

JILL: Yes.

EMMA: When you started to come out, did you know what was happening?

JILL: I was scared to go from the cave.

EMMA: What did you think you were going to find, when you came out?

JILL: Going to find out what my mom looked like.

"If a child is to keep alive her inborn sense of wonder, without any such gift from the fairies, she needs the companionship of at least one adult who can share it, rediscover with her the joy, excitement, and mystery we live in."

– Rachael Carson

Donna, age 7, China

EMMA: So, anything you say is right. There are no wrong answers. So where do you think the very first mommy came from?

DONNA: [*shrugging shoulders*] I don't know.

EMMA: Okay, you don't have to know. What about where you were? Where did you come from?

DONNA: From my mommy's tummy.

EMMA: Where were you before your mommy's tummy? It can be anything.

DONNA: I'm a little dot I think.

EMMA: Yeah? What would that feel like … being a little dot?

DONNA: Lonely.

EMMA: What color would it be?

DONNA: White.

EMMA: Lonely and white …

DONNA: … and gray.

EMMA: … and gray. Do you remember wanting to come out of there? Did you like it in there?

DONNA: Yeah.

EMMA: Both?

DONNA: [*nodding for yes*]

EMMA: And what about before you were in your mommy's
           tummy?

DONNA: [*shrugging*] I don't know.

EMMA: So, let's imagine you're in a little spaceship and
           you go off. And where would you go to?

DONNA: Mars.

EMMA: And then once you're on Mars, where would you
           go?

DONNA: Don't know.

EMMA: Any place, there's no wrong answer.

DONNA: To the sand place.

EMMA: It's sandy? And what does it look like? What are the
           colors?

DONNA: Like beige and gold and a bit of red.

EMMA: Are there any other people there?

DONNA: No.

EMMA: Are you there though?

DONNA: Yeah.

EMMA: And are you alone?

DONNA: No.

EMMA: Who's with you?

DONNA: My whole family.

EMMA: Ah. And do they look the same as they looked on Earth?

DONNA: Yes.

EMMA: If I gave you a magic wand and you could do any-thing with the magic wand to save the planet, to save Earth, what would you do?

DONNA: I think I would turn the whole world full of fresh air and all animals are in each place that we live and there are many vegetables, plants in the yard and farm.

"George Misch's analysis of the sense of wonder as expressed in the writings of early cultures in India, China, and Greece, wonder emerges as a sense of the cosmic. Wonder is in fact the cosmic sense at the stage of questioning in any language, and primary forms of questioning strongly resemble the cosmic questioning of the child.

"The aim of the cosmic questioning of both philosopher and the child is to obtain, perceptually or verbally, some reflexive action from the external world of the self, in order to understand the world in terms of his own experience as well as through the cultural explanations. For the individual these are true acts of genesis in the creation of his personal world image. Human childhood can be generalized as a highly creative, perhaps the most creative phase in every human life history, a time phase shaped and framed by characteristics shared by all races, and all peoples, primitive and sophisticated."

– Edith Cobb, The Ecology of Imagination in Childhood

Eric, age 7, France

EMMA: Where do you come from?

ERIC: From Mother.

EMMA: Where were you before that?

ERIC: Under the heart.

EMMA: How was it under the heart?

ERIC: It was difficult. It was dark. I heard Mama talk.

EMMA: What did Mama say?

ERIC: "Will it take long until my baby comes?"

EMMA: Did you talk with Mama when you were under her heart?

ERIC: No, because everything was closed.

EMMA: How was it there?

ERIC: I would have loved to talk with Mama, but it was not so bad that I could not.

EMMA: What did you want to say to Mama?

ERIC: I do not know.

EMMA: Where were you before you were under the heart?

ERIC: I think I was with Jesus.

EMMA: How was it?

ERIC: Very beautiful.

EMMA: What did Jesus look like?

ERIC: Normal size of a man.

EMMA: Where were you before you were with Jesus?

ERIC: I think a long way up in heaven.

EMMA: How was it there?

ERIC: Dark. I could not see anything. During the day it was like early morning. It was half-dark.

EMMA: Where were you before it was half-dark?

ERIC: Maybe not of this world. I was like air.

EMMA: What did it feel like to be like air?

ERIC: I was light. I could fly around everywhere.

EMMA: What is the difference between then and now?

ERIC: Now I cannot fly anymore.

EMMA: Why not?

ERIC: I am much too heavy. I am really here.

EMMA: What does it feel like to be really here?

ERIC: I am happy.

EMMA: Did you have friends in the air?

ERIC: Yes, they were also like air.

EMMA: Where were you before the air?

ERIC: I was always the air.

EMMA: What is it like to be air?

ERIC: I could see my friends but they could not see me.

EMMA: How long were you in the air?

ERIC: Two million years.

EMMA: Why did you leave the air?

ERIC: To be born.

EMMA: How?

ERIC: I floated through the window, my mother inhaled me into her heart.

EMMA: Why did you go through the window?

ERIC: I wanted to become a real man. I could make myself small and I decided to live in my mother. I liked her best.

EMMA: Can you become air again?

ERIC: Only when I die.

EMMA: What happens when you die?

ERIC: My heart stops beating, then I am in the grave. If I find a hole in the grave then I can come back out again.

EMMA: What happens after you go back to air?

ERIC: Then I go to air for eternity forever.

EMMA: What do you do in the air?

ERIC: I play with my friends and I learn to write.

EMMA: Why did you come under your mother's heart?

ERIC: Because I like life on Earth and I could meet more children. In air, I would call out to them … but they could not hear or see me.

"The most sophisticated people I know – inside they are children."

– Jim Henson

Anton, age 11, Russia

EMMA: Where do you think the sun comes from?

ANTON: It is in another planet system.

EMMA: What is that other system like?

ANTON: It is great space, containing planets that are like Earth.

EMMA: So, how did the sun get started?

ANTON: It is part of a larger sun.

EMMA: What happened to the larger sun?

ANTON: It might have exploded, and pieces turned into planets, and into the sun.

EMMA: Where did the bigger sun come from?

ANTON: An even bigger sun.

EMMA: Where did the first sun come from?

ANTON: A small planet started growing and picking up particles, and it became the first sun.

EMMA: Why did the planet grow?

ANTON: Just like all living creatures, it grew.

EMMA: What makes them grow?

ANTON: I don't know.

EMMA: Where did you come from?

ANTON: From my mother.

EMMA: Where were you before you were born?

ANTON: I didn't exist at all.

EMMA: How did the first people get started?

ANTON: People who were investigating the galaxy to decide on the best planet chose our planet.

EMMA: Did all the people start at once?

ANTON: They all landed on different parts of the planet, and when their home planet exploded, they stayed here forever.

EMMA: Are the very first people still alive?

ANTON: No, a new generation has appeared.

EMMA: When did you get started?

ANTON: Eleven years ago.

EMMA: These people from another planet, why did they come to Earth?

ANTON: They searched for a new planet because there was a shortage of air on their planet.

EMMA: How did those people get started?

ANTON: An animal gave birth to them.

EMMA: What was the animal like?

ANTON: The animal looked like a monkey.

EMMA: What started the whole process? What got nature
          started?

ANTON: It was just the time for thinking creatures to appear,
          through the process of time.

EMMA: How did time get started?

ANTON: It came of something very, very unusual. It resem-
          bles life.

EMMA: What do you mean when you say life?

ANTON: Life like a creature but not in the form of a creature,
          like air.

EMMA: Have you ever seen this creature?

ANTON: I have never seen this creature, but everyone feels
          it, inside, everywhere, all human beings feel it.

EMMA: What is it like when you feel it?

ANTON: Everything is moved by this force, when people are
          born, when they die, people are moved by this
          force.

EMMA: Do you feel this force moving you?

128

ANTON: Well, I am growing, and I was born out of this
          force.

EMMA: Can you sometimes go against the force or resist it,
          or are you always going with the force?

ANTON: The force, life, is always with me, it accompanies
          me. It is very friendly, and I can't remember ever
          having or wanting to go against it.

EMMA: Where is the force going? What is it moving to-
          ward?

ANTON: People are born, they die, and then they are born
          again. Everything moves in circles with the force.

EMMA: Will you be born again after you die?

ANTON: Yes, it will happen.

EMMA: What will it be like?

ANTON: I will not be born again instantly. I will be a trans-
          parent substance and watch the life for a while.
          When the time comes, I will appear on the earth
          once again, but before that time, I will just be in the
          sky, watching everything that is happening on the
          earth.

EMMA: Why do you come to earth and have a body?

ANTON: I would want to become a human again because I would know where the faults are, and I could help people and make some corrections. I would like that there would not be different nations, and that everyone would live together, speak the same language, and there would be a circle of friendship around the globe, and there would be no weapons.

EMMA: Why are there separations between countries, and why are there weapons?

ANTON: This is not really what the people want, but it is the wish of the United States government.

EMMA: Why do they want it?

ANTON: They are after wealth and they would like to get more countries.

EMMA: What does the life force try to do to these people, the heads of the state? What is the relationship between the life force and these people?

ANTON: These people hate the life force because they are trying to destroy it with weapons. It is impossible to convince them that it doesn't make any sense to collect so many weapons and stockpiles, but people in the long run will make the grandest transactions and deeds to show them this.

EMMA: What will you do?

ANTON: If I could, I would destroy all of the weapons and
             turn the globe into one nation, and then there would
             be friendship.

"Childhood is the name of the world's immediate future; of such, and such alone, is the promise of the kingdom of man."

– Walter De La Mare, Early One Morning

Alex, age 8, China

EMMA: So, it's just a game, just an imagination game. There are no wrong answers. Anything is right. It's not like school, wrong or right. Nothing like that. It's just fun imagination. What's your name?

ALEX: Alex.

EMMA: And how old are you?

ALEX: Eight.

EMMA: And where are you from?

ALEX: I'm from America.

EMMA: And where do you live now?

ALEX: China.

EMMA: Nice. And where do you think you came from?

ALEX: I'm born from America, but I live in China all my life.

EMMA: Okay, and before you were in China, or before you were in America where did you come from?

ALEX: My mom's ... um, my mom.

EMMA: And if you could remember what it was like inside your mom's tummy?

ALEX: I can.

EMMA: What was it like?

ALEX: It was dark.

EMMA: Yeah.

ALEX: And, like, there was a little light somewhere but I couldn't find it.

EMMA: But were you looking?

ALEX: Yeah.

EMMA: Could you hear anything in there?

ALEX: No.

EMMA: But you were looking for a light?

ALEX: Yeah.

EMMA: Do you remember wanting to come out or stay in there?

ALEX: I wanted to come out.

EMMA: You did? And so, can you remember where you were before you were inside your mommy's tummy?

ALEX: No.

EMMA: Well, what if you could? Imagination.

ALEX: Then I'll be the world's first rememberer-of-before-

134

they-were-born kid.

EMMA: So let's imagine that you are. What was it like?

ALEX: Um, maybe, maybe the air. I don't know.

EMMA: What was it like being in the air?

ALEX: Like I could do anything.

EMMA: Yeah. And were there other people with you there?
          Were you alone?

ALEX: Only feathers and stuff. They were useless.

EMMA: What were the colors of the feathers?

ALEX: Um, any color.

EMMA: Just any color. What do they feel like?

ALEX: Hard.

EMMA: Hard feathers? Oh, okay. And was there any light
          there?

ALEX: [nodding for yes]

EMMA: What did the light look like?

ALEX: Umm. A pretty light. I don't know. That light is
          coming from everywhere.

EMMA: Hmm. And it was just like endless light?

ALEX: Yeah.

EMMA: And what if you knew where you came from before you were in that light, before that infinity light?

ALEX: I don't know, but I'd like to know.

EMMA: Well, let's imagine you do know because you have a magic wand and anything is right. So, what would it be like?

ALEX: Everything is free.

EMMA: Mmmm. What does that feel like?

ALEX: You can do anything you want.

EMMA: Yeah. And so, let's imagine you are there. Everything is free. What do you want to do?

ALEX: Ummm. I want to do homework.

EMMA: Mmm. Okay. You like homework?

ALEX: Yeah.

EMMA: Cool.

ALEX: I don't like video games.

EMMA: Nice. Why don't you like video games?

ALEX: It's so boring.

EMMA: So, let's imagine you have a magic wand and you could do anything to make the world a better place.

What would you do? How would you do it?

ALEX: I would flood the whole Earth.

EMMA: Oh, wow. Okay. And flood it with?

ALEX: Um. Noah. Just make the whole Earth water for half an hour.

EMMA Ah. And what would that do?

ALEX: Destroy everything that is bad-looking or bad.

EMMA: Ahh. And then what would happen after you destroy everything with water?

ALEX: I'll rebuild everything and I'll make the environment better.

EMMA: Oh. How would you do that?

ALEX: I don't know. With my magic wand.

EMMA: Okay, well what would you do with the magic wand?

ALEX: I'll tell it to change the whole world and the environment.

"As I look back on fully seventy years of aware-
ness and recall the moments of greatest happi-
ness, they were for the most part, moments when
I lost myself all but completely in some instant of
perfect harmony. In consciousness this was due
not to me but to the non-me, of which I was
scarcely more than the subject in the grammati-
cal sense ... In childhood and boyhood this ec-
stasy overtook me when I was happy and out-
doors. Was I five or six? Certainly not seven. It
was a morning in early summer. A silver haze
shimmered and trembled over the lime trees. The
air was laden with their fragrance. The tempera-
ture was like a caress. I remember – I need not
recall – that I climbed up a tree stump and felt
suddenly immersed in Itness. I did not call it by a
name. I had no need for words. It and I were
one."

– Bernard Berenson, Sketch for a Self Portrait

Colin, age 8, China

EMMA: Where did the very first mother come from?

COLIN: What very first mother? My very first mother?

EMMA: Any first mother.

COLIN: Well, my very first mother was Cindy Guire.

EMMA: Where did she come from?

COLIN: She comes from Taiwan.

EMMA: And before she was in Taiwan, where did she come from?

COLIN: I actually don't know. She just said she's from Taiwan.

EMMA: Okay. And, so when you were a baby, where did you come from?

COLIN: I think the same place.

EMMA: Which was where?

COLIN: Well, the hospital that I came from was Queen Mary Hospital, but the country I came from, I already said that.

EMMA: And where were you before you were in the hospital?

COLIN: In my mum's tummy.

EMMA: And if you could remember what it was like in your mom's tummy, what was it like in there?

COLIN: Well, it was very squishy.

EMMA: Okay, and what would the squishiness feel like?

COLIN: Squishy. Well, from one to ten, I think it would be like one and a half.

EMMA: One and a half of squishiness. And if you could see colors, what would the colors be?

COLIN: I think I could only see black because ... I could only see black because my eyes weren't open. I think my eyes weren't open, because I wasn't that strong, so I couldn't really lift my eyelids, because I wasn't that strong, so yeah.

EMMA: Okay, yeah. And, so before you were inside of there, where did you come from? Before you were inside of your mom's squishy place?

COLIN: I came from my mom's tummy.

EMMA: Okay, but before that.

COLIN: What?! Um, I think just a blob. Just a blob.

EMMA: Okay, and before a blob?

COLIN: What?! [*pausing*] A tiny, teensy, weensy, microscopic dot.

EMMA: Okay, before that.

COLIN: What?!

EMMA: Before that.

COLIN: Okay, this is getting very far.

EMMA: Yes.

COLIN: I don't know that much about myself. I'm only eight years old, so I think that that's it.

EMMA: Okay. And remember it's imagination. So, you don't have to know the right answers. So, anything you can imagine.

COLIN: Well, I know that, um, I was fed from milk from my mom, but ... I know that. But when I wasn't drinking milk from my mom, I feel like I was just ugh, "I wish I could get out of this place. Oh my god. This is so boring. Oh my god." And I think my very first words .... like very first words, very first words was "wa" or "poof."

EMMA: Wow. Okay.

COLIN: I don't know that much about myself because I'm only eight and I'm very forgetful.

EMMA: Now, if you had a magic wand, and you could bring world peace, how would you do it with a magic wand?

COLIN: Well first I would bring back all of the people who brought world peace … Mahatma Gandhi, Malala, John F. Kennedy … no, that's a president … um, something King Junior, what is it?

EMMA: Martin Luther King

COLIN: Martin Luther King Junior?

EMMA: Yes.

COLIN: And I'd also bring back Rosa Parks and everyone. And the second thing that I would do, I would tell them about what's happening all over the world and I would ask them, "Can you help me? And can you help other people too?" And then if they helped, if they said yes, then I would be very happy.

EMMA: And how would they help you? Let's imagine how would they help.

COLIN: They would help me with … I don't know how to explain it … but they would help, they would help with, like, the Taliban; Malala would help me with the Taliban, and I feel like my teacher told me that, my teacher Ms. Smith, she told me that there are still a few people, there are still a tiny bit of people that think that it's still, that there's still, um, rights for white people and black people, and like the things that they did when Martin Luther King Junior and Rosa Parks was there ... I think, my teacher, Ms. Smith, my grade two teacher, she told me there is still people like that in a few countries only.

EMMA: Your magic wand still keeps going. And then what?

COLIN: Well, then, when we are all finished, I would celebrate and I would put on the celebratory good times song and then I would, if my wand had a tiny bit more power, I would send them back and I would also create an i-portal and at school one of the classes, they had an assembly and an i-portal is basically, you can bring people back from time and I would create an i-portal so they could come back whenever there was no world peace.

EMMA: Whenever they are needed? So, let's imagine you could do that. And then what?

COLIN: Well after everything's over, tomorrow I would ask myself what have I learned from those people? What have I learned from them? And what have I learned before that happened? And I would ask myself again and again and again. For the rest of my

143

life if I remembered, because I have bad memory already so that a thousand times, no, wait, is it two or three ... nevermind.

EMMA: It's Okay. Wow.

COLIN: I'm kind of shy.

EMMA: But you know a lot. You have a lot of wisdom. And so, you would just keep asking yourself and reminding yourself about what they told you?

COLIN: [*nods for yes*]

EMMA: Would you share them with other people so they could teach?

COLIN: Yes, I would recommend this. Okay, if there was such a thing as making messages to aliens, like translating English or any language into alien language, I would tell that to the aliens.

EMMA: What would you tell the aliens?

COLIN: That there are people on Earth, a long time ago, when your ancestors were on whatever planet they're on, when your ancestors were there and they were, and I thought that they were, and I was just very tiny, and I wasn't even born then, and I would tell them that those people, my teacher has talked to me about that, and there's this thing on Earth called school and my teacher – a person who helps you with learning – my teacher told me that there are people, Rosa Parks, Martin Luther King Junior, and Malala, and so on and so forth and I would tell that to them, to the aliens.

EMMA: And then what would the aliens do with that information?

COLIN: I think they would just ignore me and say, "Who cares about that stuff? We already have modern technology. We don't even care about that stuff. We're aliens. We're *awesomer* than humans. And they would just ignore. That's what I think. I think they would just ignore because I feel like aliens, they wouldn't listen to humans, um, because they wouldn't believe that because maybe they are not telling the truth. But actually I was telling the truth.

EMMA: And so, you really want them to understand that?

COLIN: Yes, and I want them to listen, and not ignore it.

EMMA: Yes. Because, if they really understood it, what could they do, how could they help?

COLIN: They could help by taking care of other planets and if there were different things that, um different message things that could message stuff to other planets, I wish they could do that. Like, send that message to different planets until the whole entire space system would be free of bad people … the Taliban, the white people who thought that there were black rights and white rights and whites were better than black because I thought it was very unfair.

EMMA: So, what else? Would you do anything else with your magic wand? Do you ever see aliens?

COLIN: [*shaking his head for no*] No. But, I've seen them in movies.

EMMA: Do you feel like they exist?

COLIN: Well, I think there's a teensy, weensy, tiny weensy bit of me that thinks [that] there is such a thing as aliens. Only a tiny bit. So…

EMMA: So, what else would you like to say? Anything else? It's wonderful.

COLIN: Well, I would like to say thank you to you behind the camera and yeah. Goodbye. Good day.

EMMA: Thank you so much. You are very, very wise. Thank you.

"Our birth is but a sleep and a forgetting:

The soul that rises with us, our life's Star,

Hath had elsewhere its setting,

and cometh from afar:

Not in entire forgetfulness,

and not in utter nakedness,

but trailing clouds of glory do we come

from God who is our home:

Heaven lies about us in our infancy!

Shades of the prison house begin to close

Upon the growing Boy

But he beholds the light, and whence it flows

He sees it in his joy

The Youth, who daily farther from the east

Must travel, still is nature's priest,

And by the vision splendid

Is on his way attended;

At length the Man perceives it die away,

and fade into the light of common day."

– William Wordsworth, Ode on Intimations of
Immortality from Recollections of Early
Childhood

Gail, age 10, China

EMMA: Okay, so there's only right answers. There's no
             wrong answers. So, let's imagine where were you
             before you were inside your mommy?

GAIL: With God.

EMMA: So, you were with God. Can you remember what
             that was like?

GAIL: No.

EMMA: Okay, and what about before you were with God?

GAIL: I wasn't here.

EMMA: So what if you can imagine where the very first
             mommy came from, or mother. Where did the very
             first mother come from?

GAIL: From God too.

EMMA: Okay, she came from God. And where was she be-
             fore God?

GAIL: Probably in the sky. Kind of hovering.

EMMA: What was it like for the mother to be hovering
             around? What was she doing? What was it like for
             her?

GAIL: Um, I think she was really curious about her surroundings. She wants to explore what there is.

EMMA: So, she kind of wants to explore. Do you have any
           sense of where she was before she wanted to ex-
           plore? Before she was hovering, where was she?

GAIL: I don't think she was there.

EMMA: So, when she was hovering, was she all alone?
           Were there others with her?

GAIL: One other person.

EMMA: Who was the other person with her?

GAIL: A man.

EMMA: Okay, so they are hovering, kind of there. And then
           what happened?

GAIL: God sent them to Earth.

EMMA: Okay, and how do they come to Earth?

GAIL: They fly.

EMMA: So they fly to Earth. And what is it like for them?
           The very first mother, and is he a father? Or is he
           just a man?

GAIL: He's a father.

EMMA: So, what was that like for them to be the very first
           mother and father on Earth?

GAIL: It was quite strange, and a bit mysterious. They
           didn't really know anything. So, they have to find
           knowledge themselves and experience things.

EMMA: How did they find knowledge themselves? How did
           they do that?

GAIL: They probably experienced a lot of dangerous
           things and they learned. Like maybe some plants
           were, like, poisonous, so they learned to stay away.
           And also, they might learn to stay away from preda-
           tors to be safe.

EMMA: And then once they learn that, what do they do with
           that knowledge?

GAIL: They pass it on so other people don't have to find
           out for themselves.

EMMA: Because they tell them. Yeah. And then what do
           they do? There they are on Earth and they flew
           there. Do they still have wings while they are walk-
           ing around? How is that?

GAIL: They are like humans.

EMMA: So, did they lose their wings when they came to
           Earth?

GAIL: [Nods her head yes.]

150

EMMA: And then where did the first baby come from?

GAIL: From God.

EMMA: And how did God decide, you know, where the very
            first baby would be born?

GAIL: Maybe because he knows the baby's conditions, and
            so then he knows what the baby should experience,
            and what is too dangerous for it, for now. So, for
            example, he might not send the baby to Syria now
            because there is a war there, and the baby is too
            young to die. He might send it to another country
            because it's a safe place with a lot of supplies.

EMMA: So, each baby has a special kind of place wherever
            they end up.

GAIL: [nodding for yes]

EMMA: And so, do you have a sense of why you came to
            your parents? Your mom?

GAIL: I think it's because God decided that I would be bet-
            ter in a safe place, instead of a war zone or a really
            dangerous place. And he sent me here for a reason,
            instead of … like he could have picked any other
            place in the world, but he picked here.

EMMA: So, if you could know why God sent you here,
            what's the reason?

GAIL:	Um, God thinks that I could cope more with the sur-rounding instead of someplace else. He thinks I could have more chances and relationships here.
EMMA:	So, it would be better for you here? Do you have any sense of what your purpose is for being here? To give to the world?
GAIL:	Yeah, like there are other role models as well, like teachers, like Mother Teresa, so then I think my purpose is to help the less fortunate and to give them their basic needs and, like, help refugees and so on.
EMMA:	So, you seem to know that already? Do you have a plan to make that happen or to work toward that?
GAIL:	Well, my parents donate to these charities, and in [the] future I'm thinking of opening my own charity to help.
EMMA:	To help the world? To help refugees? That's won-derful.
GAIL:	Because there are a lot of refugees that have to es-cape from really bad conditions. And one third of the entire population of the world is refugees.
EMMA:	Oh, I didn't know that.

GAIL: Well, 65 million people are refugees.

EMMA: Wow. I didn't know that. Thank you for sharing
            that. That's hard isn't it?

GAIL: And I'm not sure if every one of them has had a
            chance and found a new home, so I feel bad for
            them.

EMMA: So, you feel you can help give them a new chance
            and give them hope?

GAIL: I could start a new business and I could give them
            jobs and education, so then they can pay their actual
            rent to other people who are less fortunate.

EMMA: That makes sense. That's a good idea. So, what
            could you do if you had a magic wand to create
            world peace? What would you do to create world
            peace?

GAIL: Well, first of all, I wouldn't really want other peo-
            ple conflicting because that affects a lot of busi-
            nesses, and the governments just think about them-
            selves and they don't care about how their decisions
            affect businesses and also, I think governments and
            companies should be more accepting. They should
            invest money in helping others instead of being re-
            ally selfish and just trying to keep all of the money

for themselves. So, I think world peace is really good because that just brings harmony into our world and we wouldn't have wars and it would do good for our air and our land as well, because if there's a war, all bombs kind of destroy the buildings and you have to cut down more trees to build more homes. It's not very good for the environment.

EMMA: Right. Kind of like a bad cycle. What other things would you do to help the environment with a magic wand?

GAIL: Well, I want for people to not throw trash into the sea because it just doesn't help the animals and also to stop cutting down trees; like not as much trees because people cut down too many trees and they get extra paper but you're still destroying animals' homes, and also for people to not throw trash on the floor or on the beach because it pollutes the air and for us to use reusable objects like glass containers or plastic containers so we don't waste as much because plastic can't disintegrate as well as some other things.

EMMA: Even rebuying clothes, reusing clothes ... that's another way to do it too.

GAIL: Also, we have these boxes here where you can put
            your old clothes to donate them. I don't really do
            that because I usually give my old clothes to my
            relatives.

EMMA: Well, that's perfect. You're still recycling. That's
            great. So, let's imagine you're in a spaceship and
            you can just go out. Where would you go to?

GAIL: Um, Mars. Because right now ... I don't know
            which scientist, but one of my teachers showed me
            ... we might need to move to Mars because of all
            the problems we have caused in this world. So, I
            want to explore Mars because if we really want to
            move there we want to be prepared instead of just
            going there empty-handed without any knowledge.

EMMA: So, you'd like to know that ahead of time. Yeah,
            that makes sense. So, what about virtual reality?

GAIL: Well, I don't think it's really good. Well, I like to
            play with it. I just don't think it's very good for
            people because some people are already addicted to
            their phones and stuff, so with virtual reality, when
            it came out, they might get even more addicted to
            technology when most knowledge comes from ex-
            perience and books. Also, my teacher told me that
            this guy is in virtual reality and he was really poor

and in this virtual reality world he had a daughter and he had all the money he wanted and then he went to buy an ice-cream for his daughter and also his dog. But that was all in the virtual reality world so when he took off the thing, he found out he was still alone and he had really little money and so it kind of makes people want stuff even more and just be more selfish and greedy instead of helping others.

EMMA: Because it makes it more real even though they can't have it, but they want it more.

GAIL: They envision it even more than they have in their minds because it's just right there in front of them.

EMMA: Could there be any good reasons to have it? Could it help in any way?

GAIL: Well, I saw this virtual reality of how refugees live, and I think it helped me because I didn't know how bad the conditions were until now, and how filthy and dirty refugees were, and so virtual reality helped because it's kind of like a 3D world and then you get to kind of experience and see what refugees and other poor people are experiencing.

EMMA: So, you learned. As a learning tool it was good. But

then you don't want to get addicted to it. So, it really did help you, because now you want to help refugees. That's great. So, see if there is anything else you want to say?

GAIL: Well, I think that poverty is a bad thing and I think governments should pay attention to this more because right now everyone is just focusing on themselves and they don't think about others and people have to work really hard to achieve what they want and some people don't get their basic needs but they still want more. And none of us are willing to really help – only like a little bit. And not a lot of people try to help the animals because they just care about how they live and not about others, so I feel like our world should start to change if we don't want to kill as many creatures, because right now a lot of animals and people are dying. Like people are dying from cancer and lung disease and many others. But creatures are dying mostly from pollution and plastic and also not enough food, and no shelter.

EMMA: Yeah, being cold and not protected.

GAIL: And also, global warming. So, we should start helping the Earth more.

EMMA: And so, you have some ideas how you would do that. Would that be part of your charity? Would it be around global warming? What would you do?

GAIL: I'm not sure about how bad things would be in the future, but if I were to say I was going to own a company or charity right now, I would probably help every problem, not only just the people but also animals and the environment so then we could live a healthy life and also a good life.

EMMA: Yes. Seems like you have a really good heart and a really good mind and you really want to do this.

GAIL: Thank you.

"Nothing was more difficult for me in childhood than to admit the notion of death as a state applicable to my own being ... it was not so much from the source of animal vivacity that my difficulty came, as from a sense of indomitableness of the spirit within me ... with a feeling congenial to this, I was often unable to think of external things as having an external existence, and I communed with all that I saw as something not apart from, but inherent in, my own immaterial nature. Many times, while going to school I have grasped a wall or a tree to recall myself from the abyss of idealism to reality ... to that dreamlike vividness and splendour which invests objects of sight in childhood, everyone, I believe, if he would look back, could bear testimony ... I took hold of the notion of pre-existence as having sufficient foundation in humanity authorising me to make for my purpose the best use of it as a poet."

– William Wordsworth

Kay, age 10, China

EMMA: So, there's no wrong answers. Where do you think the very first baby came from?

KAY: Um, from a mom.

EMMA: Okay, and where do you think the very first mom came from?

KAY: God.

EMMA: Where do you think God came from?

KAY: He just appeared.

EMMA: And what do you think it was like, wherever God was? Wherever he appeared from?

KAY: It was bright. And it was full of happiness.

EMMA: Do you ever go there now? Do you know that place now?

KAY: No, I'm not sure.

EMMA: Do you ever go there in your dreams?

KAY: I think it's sort of like *your* happy spot. Like, it's different for everyone.

EMMA: That's how you feel it? Okay. If you had a magic wand and you could make any change in the world

	to make it a better place, what would you want to do?
KAY:	For everyone to stay healthy and have world peace.
EMMA:	So, if you took the wand, how would you imagine being able to do that? How could everyone stay healthy?
KAY:	With all of the hospitals. You don't have to pay for anything. You can just, like, it can be like a free act.
EMMA:	If there was complete world peace, how would you create that with your wand?
KAY:	Like, it's not really possible, because there are always disagreements. Like, two sides, so I'm not really sure.
EMMA:	But what if you just knew? What if you had magic powers?
KAY:	Then if you had no world peace, then you would always be right, which isn't always necessarily a good thing.
EMMA:	How can that not be a good thing?
KAY:	Because if you are wrong, then you can learn from your mistakes. But if you are just right you will just brag a lot about it and stuff.

EMMA: That makes sense. Any more thoughts on that?

KAY: Yeah, but because I think that world peace is when
           two people start a conflict, and if it turns into a war
           then one day the war will finish, and after the war
           finishes, one of them will agree with the other and
           then it will be peaceful for a while until the next
           conflict.

EMMA: So, we have peace, and then conflict. Is that what
           you are saying? Is there some reason for that?

KAY: I think we have conflict because without conflict
           our world would be no wrong answers and then
           everyone would agree and you wouldn't need an
           education and stuff, because there is only one an-
           swer.

EMMA: What would one answer be like? What if there was
           just one answer?

KAY: No choice.

EMMA: Ahhhh.

KAY: Like, in life, you can be whatever you want when
           you grow up. You can be a doctor, or a dentist, or
           an athlete. Then you have to do it and it would be
           hard to get jobs and stuff.

EMMA: Hmmm. So, where you do you think you came
           from?

KAY: Like, a long time ago, my great, great, great, great,
           great grandma was born from God and then got
           passed down to my mom, and then my mom had
           me.

EMMA: Do you remember any of that? Do you remember
           being inside your mommy at all?

KAY: No, not really.

EMMA: Do you remember being before you were inside
           your mommy?

KAY: Some people believe, like I have seen YouTube
           videos about people remembering their past life and
           it's really freaky because they thought they were
           like a famous horse rider or something, but they
           were just an average kid going to a school and some
           people believe in past lives. I don't think I do. I
           don't remember having a past life at all.

EMMA: So, what if you were to remember where you were
           before you came into your mommy?

KAY: That would be weird. Like I'd ask if I had the same
           parents first, where I lived, what my name would

be, what school I would go to and stuff. And if I
was human.

EMMA: So, does all of that seem possible? Maybe? Or not?

KAY: It could be possible. I think it's possible for some
           people and some people, they just started.

EMMA: Say more about that. What do you mean, they just
           started?

KAY: Like, it's their first life.

EMMA: Ah. Yes.

KAY: It's like those video games. You have five lives and
           if you use them all then you die.

EMMA: Ah. And then you die and then what?

KAY: I think, because, a lot of people who believe in faith
           and stuff, they believe in heaven and hell and think
           after you use those lives, you go to one of those.

EMMA: You go to either heaven or hell?

KAY: [nodding for yes]

EMMA: Is there anything besides heaven or hell? Is there
           anything beyond that?

KAY: I'm not necessarily Christian because my parents
           aren't, but you can just stay in a coffin. Like a

164

blank... I'm not sure, but like your dream world.

EMMA: What's your dream world like?

KAY: When I'm older, I want to be a horse trainer because I'm really into it and so I guess my dream world would be one with lots of horses.

EMMA: That makes you happy! I can tell that.

KAY: Yeah.

EMMA: So, you know that's what you want to do? You want to be with, be around horses?

KAY: Yeah.

EMMA: And so, if you had another magic wand and you could do anything to make the world so climate change wasn't going on ...

KAY: I'd make sure that no sin can come into the world.

EMMA: So just stop it from the very beginning?

KAY: But I was thinking twice about that because if there's no sin, there's no conflict, then we don't need an education and then there's no choice. So, maybe not.

EMMA: So, it seems like we need choice.

KAY: Yeah, choice is really important because choice is
                where you get a chance. Like, everybody has a dif-
                ferent opinion on what their chance will be.

EMMA: Do you have a sense of what your chance will be?

KAY: When I'm old, I want to be a horse trainer.

EMMA: That's exciting. Can you see it happening?

KAY: Yeah, because my great, great, great grandfather
                went to the Olympics. So it got passed on through
                generations.

EMMA: I feel that! That's exciting that you know that.

"Blessed be Childhood, which brings down something of Heaven into the midst of our rough earthiness."

– Henri Frederic Amiel

Andy, age 10, Switzerland

*When I first interviewed Andy, the teacher explained he most likely would not give a good interview as he struggled in school and was barely passing his classes.

EMMA: Where do you come from?

ANDY: Yeek! From mommy.

EMMA: What was it like in mommy?

ANDY: All black.

EMMA: How did it feel?

ANDY: Soft.

EMMA: Where were you before you were with mommy?

ANDY: I was small and black and in the air.

EMMA: And what was that like?

ANDY: Beautiful.

EMMA: Were you alone in the air?

ANDY: [*laughing*] No, there were other people, friends in the air.

EMMA: What were you doing in the air?

ANDY: We ran and floated in the air.

EMMA: Where were you before the air?

ANDY: I think, I was really nothing, not the air, nothing.

EMMA: What was it like?

ANDY: Like nothing!

EMMA: Were you alone in nothing?

ANDY: Yes, very alone.

EMMA: What happened to the friends that were in the air
            with you?

ANDY: They were also nothing once they were in nothing.

EMMA: Are you nothing or something now?

ANDY: My brother told me I was made of these little parti-
            cles that go through me and I do not agree! I feel
            like something because I can hit myself and it hurts.
            So I'm something.

EMMA: Do you feel like nothing, now?

ANDY: [*laughing*] Yes, only in my dreams.

EMMA: Often in your dreams?

ANDY: Yes.

EMMA: Do you like it?

ANDY: No, well yes, at times in dreams I am nothing, and
            that feels very good, because I can look at the earth

from my dreams. It is very beautiful, yet at the same moment it isn't. This is the wonderful side. The bad thing about nothing is that I cannot have real friends in nothing. Yet, because I am not on the earth in nothing, and only in my dreams, I cannot play games, yet at the same time, I can look everywhere, and see everything. That's the only thing, one can see everything and that is the only thing about nothing, that is beautiful. But the other thing is that we have a choice to see nothing or something.

EMMA: What is the difference between nothing and the air?

ANDY: In the air one can touch. The air gives resistance, if you take a towel and move it, you can feel the air. And when I'm in nothing, the air cannot get me cold. But I can blow at the air, but air cannot blow at me. When I am in the nothing, the air cannot touch me.

EMMA: When do you become the air?

ANDY: First you are in nothing, where you see everything. Then you spend four years in nothing and then four years in the air. Then you go in the body of your mommy for four years, then you are started and spend more months in mommy, then you are born.

EMMA: When you are in the air and waiting four years, are
            there others with you?

ANDY: Yes, there are others.

EMMA: What do they look like?

ANDY: Same as me?

EMMA: What is that like?

ANDY: Because everyone is similar in the air, it makes a
            very big friendship, there is no separation.

EMMA: What happens when you leave the air?

ANDY: We wait four years.

EMMA: Then what?

ANDY: Because in the air we cannot hit each other, so we
            are all friends. Then I choose my mother because I
            think she is well and best for me and then I go to
            her.

EMMA: Do all of the others go to mothers as well?

ANDY: Yes, they all go and look for mothers.

EMMA: How do they come down, if there is no separation?

ANDY: There is a moment of separation. At this moment,
            all separate, except if they are twins, then they go

171

together to mommy. If not, everyone goes their own way.

EMMA: Do they ever get back together?

ANDY: No, when the time in the air is over, and after we get to know each other in the air, it then is the end of air, and we become strangers. Then when we are down and come out of our mommies and are separated from the air and each other ... then later we go to school, maybe we may recognize someone from air. But usually it is not in the first moment that we will find and recognize an air person. It may be later, that we may remember that a person was once with us in the air ... and then that can be true friendship. And if you become friends and hit each other, now it will hurt because we are no longer in the air. Now it is possible to feel pain.

EMMA: Why do we separate and leave the air and come into bodies?

ANDY: Because we cannot all go to the same mommy. It would be too much for one mommy, too much pain, so we must separate. We are sleeping in the mommy and one day before we are born, we may lose memory of these things and being in the air. That is why sometimes it is hard to find each other again once we are born.

EMMA: Why don't we just stay in the air? Why do we get born?

ANDY: If you stay too long in the air (it's special air, it's not the same as we breathe here) then all of a sudden you cannot breathe anymore, you will die if you stay too long in the air. You have to take a body to really breathe the air, the air we have down here lets you breathe for longer.

EMMA: Is there a reason or purpose we take a body?

ANDY: To become whole. We come to do things. To eat, to work, and to breathe.

EMMA: How do we get into our mommies?

ANDY: As I said before, when the four years are over, we become very long and thin and we are able to enter the skin of mommy. I go to sleep in mommy and I wake up before I am born.

EMMA: Can we go back to nothing?

ANDY: Only in our dreams.

EMMA: Do we ever go back to the air?

173

ANDY: It's a circle, when I die, I go back and become an angel, then to air, then to nothing, then it all happens all over again.

EMMA: Where are the angels?

ANDY: Angels are everywhere.

EMMA: Are they in nothing?

ANDY: There are no angels in nothing. If there is a mistake, and an angel goes there too fast, then the angel will be thrown out as quickly as it entered.

EMMA: What is a mistake?

ANDY: When you have no patience and you cannot wait. If you are an angel and you go too quickly into the nothing state, then you have to wait longer, and more pains are put on you, and the circle starts again. Whoever goes too quickly has to wait. If you can wait, then you are free to go to nothing. There are leaders, like kings, in every state. The leader is responsible to see that things go okay. If some beings are going too quick, they add things to them to make them stay longer.

EMMA: What is the leader like?

174

ANDY: Externally he looks exactly the same as the others, but sometimes, the leader may have a longer arm, or a halo. The leader is only to help us learn patience, then we do not have to experience so much pain.

*After the interview with Andy, the interpreter said she was so moved by Andy's interview that she wanted to share it with his teacher. She did; the teacher was shocked as she thought he had lower intelligence based on his grades. The teacher confirmed she doubted he had learned his concepts of what he believed from his parents. They were working class. The interpreter was so moved to learn this that she was curious to follow Andy for a little over a year and learned he had raised his grades to excellent. His interview had been shared with the principal and he was viewed differently and given more attention.

*"How can I accept a limited definable self,
when I feel, in me, all possibilities?"*

– Anais Nin

Fifty Years Later...
Brett, age 53, Los Angeles, CA

Questions via text, June 2018

EMMA: I am curious if you remember us being close when you were young at age four and if you remember me?

BRETT: Unfortunately, I am one of those children who does not have a good memory. In fact, most of my childhood through high school even is more of a jigsaw puzzle than a timeline of memories. I have fragments of memories, more visual than anything, of smiling with you and warmth.

EMMA: Do you have any spiritual connection now with God, nature, or maybe religion?

BRETT: I am not connected to any organized religion, but I am a very spiritual person. I compose music and get immense joy from it. When music is at its best, I know that there is a bigger picture than me. I would not call it God, but something. I am a serious student of religion and history. Fascinated by it honestly. The story of how the Bible came to be in its current form is one of my favorite subjects. I am definitely not religious, but I do take the stories and the words and incorporate the best of them into my life. I am just a bit too much of a realist to believe in something I cannot explain. I view things more in the context of quantum physics than any one religion. I could go on for days about how religions have altered human life. I am not anti-religion, I am just anti-the people that run them I guess. Interesting that we would talk about that. I was always a bit precocious and never knew quite where religion fit for me.

BRETT: After 50 years, are we having the same conversation?

EMMA: Do you want to see the interview from when you were four years old that you told me and my mom?

BRETT: I would love to read it ASAP.

EMMA: I will take a photo. It's very short but stayed with me my whole life. You wanted to talk about our spiritual connection and you had so much to say about wisdom and knew where we came from.

BRETT: I do have a memory of sitting with you in church but thought it was my sister, but never felt right.

EMMA: Yes, you would always come sit with me at church.

[I text Brett a photo of his interview that is the first of the inter-

views in Part Two of this book.]

BRETT: I am overwhelmed.

EMMA: I know: breathe. Our connection and our conversa-
            tions played a huge role in my life. I have collected
            interviews from kids in different countries that
            demonstrate their inner wisdom too. I think you will
            enjoy reading it.

            I was so happy today that you had a memory of my
            smile and warmth. It made me weep. I was thrilled
            to learn and know you remained Brett as I knew you
            at your core.

[After reading his interview at age four.]

BRETT: I swear I almost remember this. There is something
            so familiar. I can't quite touch it, but I have always
            had a fascination about the eyes. I do not like the
            telephone to this day as I cannot see a person's
            eyes. In my dreams people do not talk; there is no
            need. I mean "Wow!" This is me; I can feel it is
            right. My memory is not good because I do not see
            things in a timeline but know deep down that I nev-

179

er truly forget anything. I would love to read your entire book. What a fascinating study. I am going to take a walk I think. I will talk to you soon.

*"Accept the children the way we accept trees –
with gratitude, because they are a blessing – but
do not have expectations or desires. You don't
expect trees to change, you love them as they
are."*

– Isabel Allende

The Golden Key

So, what is the magic and wonderment of our Divine Child and of childhood?

The magic comes when we are children because we are in the moment. We have access to wisdom, because we are present. Here lies the Golden Key from my dream when I was four years old. The Golden Key is for all of us, for everyone. The Golden Key is Pure Love and Pure Presence. Please take the Golden Key and unlock your door to be fully present so that we all might truly have a Servant's Heart.

The Children of the Earth are calling us to wake up and be present, so that we might serve our planet and help all of those in need. Let yourself be in the Enchanted Garden of a Servant's Heart where anything is possible; especially, the miracles that happen when we take positive actions to serve the world.

Here is a very special song and music video, composed and created by my son, Patrick Rawlings. It captures my feelings about the universe and love for serving humanity and Mother Earth. As you listen you can remember and nurture your own Divine Child. Children will love this music video too.

To access and keep this free song, please go to this link www.earthsoundmedia.com/the-divine-child and please use the promo code *thedivinechildgift* to download and keep this song in your heart forever.

What if world peace is possible?

What if we can help planet earth and all living creatures not just survive, but actually thrive?

Please take the Golden Key I am giving you and pause, be still, go within your heart and feel our one heart beating. We are one with earth, ourselves and everything. It's okay to wake up and live differently than you did the day before. It's okay to remember why we are here and take actions every day that help every living creature.

"The sole meaning of life is to serve humanity."

– Leo Tolstoy

"Children are our future, and the only way for the world to evolve, as I have been shown it should be, is for each generation to be more loving and compassionate than the one before. This is only possible if we support the children around us and protect and encourage them so that they do not lock their love away."

– Lorna Byrne

My Wish for You

My wish for you is that you start to be more aware of moments in your life that you remember from your childhood that are similar to these interviews, or experiences from when you were a child that stand out as maybe a feeling of one-ness with nature and feeling one with the world; maybe an experience of God. Or seeing or hearing things that others did not hear or see. It's okay to have a different experience than others. It's okay if you, your child or other children in your life experience godlike experiences that seem extraordinary. It's okay to believe in unicorns and it's okay to be exactly who you are. It's okay if you have had trauma, dyslexia or have seen little flying saucers. It's okay to be any sex you are. It's okay to pursue any vocation you choose. It's okay to see rainbows and to see more than rainbows. It's okay to be different; actually, let go of the idea of trying to fit in. You do not need to step into a box or a circle. It can be more interesting and fun if you don't. The only rule is to be kind to yourself and everything that breathes.

Please shine and do not keep yourself small in fear of not being normal. Please do not feel you must fit in. Moreover, with your knowing, how can you interact with children so they feel heard, understood and respected, so they never feel the need to dim their inner light, and so they move into adulthood remembering their purpose for being on this planet? How can we support children to remain the best and brightest versions of themselves throughout their lives?

Please be all of who you are so that we, collectively, might serve and save Mother Earth, the animal kingdom and humanity. Please connect to your Pure heart. Pause, breathe and remember we are here to bring peace and to live in harmony with ourselves and our neighbors. Step back, down and in.

Then, please move into action by giving more love to the children in your life, to yourself, to your family and to the community in which you live. Reach out and rescue an animal, a neighbor or a child in your life. Volunteer in a way that speaks to your heart. When we move from our heart-space and remember we have free choice and the ability to wake up, we can create real solutions for our everyday problems in the world.

We are here to help Earth not destroy her. Remember we are one.

With Gratitude,
Emma
TheDivineChild.org

"A hero is someone who has given his or her life to something bigger than oneself."

– Joseph Campbell

Referral Sources

- National Center for PTSD, www.ptsd.va.gov
- Does My Child Have Psychic Abilities? Kids and Psychic Powers, www.iacworld.org
- Healing Complex Trauma and PTSD: Inner Child Healing, https://www.healingfromcomplextraumaandptsd.com/inner-child-healing
- David Lynch Foundation, www.davidlynchfoundation.org
- Mind Up, a product of The Hawn Foundation, https://mindup.org/thehawnfoundation/
- The Yale Center for Dyslexia, http://dyslexia.yale.edu/
- 6 Steps to Help Heal Your Inner Child, https://psychcentral.com/blog/6-steps-to-help-heal-your-inner-child/
- Memories of Heaven, Dr. Wayne Dyer and Dee Garnes, www.drwaynedyer.com
- What Our Children Teach Us: Lessons in Joy, Love and Awareness, Piero Ferrucci http://pieroferrucci.it/
- Common Characteristics of Adult Dyslexia: Dyslexia The Gift, https://www.dyslexia.com/about-dyslexia/signs-of-dyslexia/common-characteristics-of-adult-dyslexia/
- Association for Comprehensive Energy Psychology, www.energypsych.org
- New Treatment for Post-Traumatic Stress Disorder Delivers Rapid, Long Lasting Results, www.emofree.com
- Stress Reduction Music, Patrick Rawlings, www.earthsoundmedia.com
- How To Handle Your Feelings. Your Gut Feeling,

Dr Quoc Vo D.O.,
http://www.youtube.com/watch?v=xJgBpFsLlG8

- Conversations with G: A Physician's Encounter with Heaven, Dr. Norman Shealy M.D., www.normshealy.com
- Cascade Hypnosis Center, Ericka Flint, https://cascadehypnosiscenter.com
- Anti-Stress Game, Champions of the Shengha, www.championsoftheshengha.com/
- Dr. Bradley Nelson, The Emotion Code, www.drbradleynelson.com
- Lorna Byrne, Angels in my Hair, https://foundation.lornabyrne.com
- Conscious Parenting News, a nonprofit initiative of Kindred World, www.consciousparentingnews.com
- Joseph Chilton Pearce, The Magical Child, www.josephchiltonpearce.org/books.html
- Bruce Lipton, The Biology of Belief, Conscious Evolution www.brucelipton.com
- Neal Rogin, Wisdom Revolution, a Marin Link program, https://www.wisdom-revolution.org/
- Nancy and Pete "Rocketman" Conrad, https://www.conradchallenge.org/
- China Galland, Love Cemetery, http://www.chinagalland.com
- Lady Diana Whitmore, Growing2gether, Ecologia Youth Trust, www.ecologia.org.uk
- Dr. Jim Tucker, Return to Life, https://med.virginia.edu/perceptual-studies/research-area/children-who-report-memories-of-previous-lives/
- Mission Be: Teaching mindfulness to educators for children, www.missionbe.org
- Lee Lipsenthal, Enjoy Every Sandwich, Living Each Day As If It Were Your Last

"There can be no keener revelation of a society's soul than the way in which it treats its children."

– Nelson Mandela

Acknowledgments

My sincere thanks to all the children in so many countries who so willingly let me ask them open-ended questions.

My gratitude and compassion for all children who witness violence of any kind. My prayer is that they too will heal and find their voice.

I would like to acknowledge God, Angels, and all that is the loving unseen and seen.

My husband, Jim, thank you for your unconditional love, support, and acceptance. My son, Patrick, your wisdom and kind heart and for always telling me (since age three) to write this book.

To Jennifer McKinley, Cynthia Kane and Sheri Hanlon, my editors. The Author Incubator, Angela Lauria. Lydia Graham, for the presence of detail. Thank you, Barbara Deal for reminding me to remember what I knew.

Thank you also Bill Gladstone at Waterside Productions.

My amazing monk doc, Quoc Vo DO, who brought me back to life after car accidents and spinal surgery. He retrieved my soul and walked me through deep PTSD memories to arrive here.

My heart is forever grateful to my childhood neighbor and soul friend, Brett. Then and now, thank you for remembering my eyes.

"We know we must leave a better world for our children, but we must also leave better children for our world."

– Nancy and Pete "Rocketman" Conrad

192

About the Author

Emma Farr Rawlings has a master's degree in clinical psychology, a master's degree in cultural anthropology, and a PhD in behavioral sciences from International College, West Los Angeles and Ryokan College. Emma was an adjunct professor at JFK University and taught Presence in Coaching. She became an ICF Master Certified Coach in 2007. She has been a consultant, coach, and trusted advisor for over 35 years in the San Francisco Bay Area, as well as internationally, serving the technology and media/music industries, spiritual leaders, eco-leaders, and VIPs in many fields. She retired her Transpersonal Psychotherapy practice of four decades in 2014, but can be found at www.thedivinechild.org.

She is currently in the midst of a project which aims to transform life for the betterment of all on this planet. Emma loves to hike with her family and her dog too.

Waterside Press